MW00416568

SEVEN LAWS WHICH GOVERN INCREASE AND ORDER

BY NEIL KENNEDY

Copyright © 2007

Neil Kennedy Ministries Group
The Ministry of Neil Kennedy
82 Plantation Pointe
Fairhope, AL 36532
www.NeilKennedyMinistries.com

Unless otherwise indicated, all Scripture quotations are taken from the Holy Bible: New International Version®, NIV®. Copyright © 1973, 1978, 1984 by International Bible Society. Used by permission of Zondervan Publishing House. All rights reserved.

Scripture quotations marked KJV are taken from the King James Version of the Bible.

Seven Laws Which Govern Increase And Order
Previously published as Grace To Grow: The Seven Laws Which Govern Divine Increase And Order
ISBN-10: 0-9777039-5-9
ISBN-13: 978-0-9777039-5-1

Original Copyright © 2004 by Neil Kennedy
Second Copyright © 2007 by Neil Kennedy
82 Plantation Pointe
Fairhope, AL 36532

Editor: Linda A. Schantz

Printed in the United States of America.
All rights reserved under International Copyright Law.
Contents and/or cover may not be reproduced in whole or in part in any form without the express written consent of the Publisher.
Neil Kennedy Ministries Group
82 Plantation Pointe, Fairhope, AL 36532,
www.NeilKennedyMinistries.com

DEDICATION

This book is dedicated to
my best friend,
lover and wife,
Kay,
and to my three incredible children,
Alexandra, Chase, and Courtney.

The Seven Laws Which Govern Increase And Order are practical and power-filled principles which have transformed the way I live and the way I run my company. By employing these truths, our customer base and influence in the community has grown beyond our stated goals in record time. I believe so strongly in the benefit of employing *The Seven Laws,* that each of our employees receives a copy of these principles at orientation. I want them to understand the principles that steer the course of our company, and to experience firsthand the life-changing impact these principles can have in their own lives.

> Kevin VanKorlaar, Ph.D., LMHC
> President and CEO
> Wisdom For Living, Inc.

The Seven Laws teaching of Neil Kennedy will bring a God-birthed passion and excitement to your congregation. Our people were extremely motivated to do God's work with excellence. Without any reservation, I highly recommend my friend Neil Kennedy. Move out of the comfort zone and invite him today!

> Brad Rosenberg
> Lead Pastor
> Tri-County Assembly
> Fairfield, Ohio

In all my travels across our fellowship, I found Neil Kennedy to be one of the most creative, hardworking and dedicated ministers that we have.

> Dan Betzer
> Senior Pastor
> First Assembly Of God
> Fort Myers, Florida

You hear much about moving from "good to great" and "taking it to the next level." There's much talk about achieving excellence. I'm convinced it is all a process. *The Seven Laws Which Govern Increase And Order,* presented to our church, helped us move forward in that process, as it presented relevant and practical steps to follow on the journey from good to great.

Ed Russo
Senior Pastor
Victorious Life Church
Tampa, Florida

TABLE OF CONTENTS

Introduction 1

1 The Law Of Seed 11

2 The Law Of Attraction 31

3 The Law Of Hospitality 47

4 The Law Of Reflex 61

5 The Law Of Mutual Benefit 75

6 The Law Of Faith To Follow 89

7 The Law Of Order 105

Grace To Grow 117

Introduction

God has equipped you for increase.

God created you with the image of increase on the inside of you when you were born again. Satan, sin, sickness and insufficiency have no unsettled claims on you. The curse that was pronounced against all mankind has been nullified through Jesus Christ. The salvation God has provided for you has both an eternal and a temporal effect. Salvation has a promise both for this present life and for the life to come (I Timothy 4:8).

Most people approach the Christian faith solely from the eternal salvation experience. Eternal salvation is certainly the core message of Christ, yet amazingly few people have actually looked into the Bible for practical answers to their daily needs. Many have a confidence in the "sweet by-and-by," but God's salvation also impacts us in the nasty here and now.

Salvation is a now experience. **The word *salvation* means *wholeness.*** Salvation encompasses every area of life. The word *salvation* also indicates, the concept of *nothing broken and nothing missing.*

Have you realized that it's God's good pleasure to see success and increase in your life?

It satisfies Him to see you succeed.

The teaching of *The Seven Laws Which Govern Increase And Order* are the culmination of years of study and practical application. My searching out these principles from God's Word was borne out of necessity.

As a child, I claimed to be a Christian but failed to practice the faith. When I became a young man, my life was filled with so much pain, lack and discouragement that I began to seek answers.

One day, in desperation, I read a self-help book hoping to find some solutions to my problems. The author was a businessman who had committed himself to reading one chapter of the Book of Proverbs every day of the month. So I also turned to the Word of God—specifically, the wisdom of Solomon in Proverbs.

Even before I accepted Jesus as my Savior I committed to reading the Book of Proverbs. *(It's fortunate that there are thirty-one chapters. That's one chapter for each day of the month.)* The practical teachings concerning every facet of life amazed me!

I began to see Christianity in a very different light. Before, I had thought of Christianity as a religion—not a living, active faith. But I found out that Christianity is not religious at all. It provides real, relevant and reliable truths that can be applied to give us sufficiency in every arena of life—spiritual, mental and physical.

Not long after I accepted Jesus as my Savior, I knew God was calling me into full-time ministry. I attended Bible college and, shortly thereafter, accepted my first position in ministry as a minister to youth. Soon I felt the Holy Spirit stirring me to plant a church in a suburb of Mobile, Alabama. My family and I stepped out in faith to start that church. The challenges I faced there as a new pastor forced me to continue my search for wisdom and practical truths.

A church is a unique organization with the purpose of propagating the Gospel. Just like any business or organization, the Church of Jesus Christ has a "product." The "product" of the Church is the Message. That's it.

To spread the Gospel to a community, a church requires enormous organizational and motivational skills. In order to reach people with its message, a church must build facilities to accommodate attendance, train and manage volunteers to properly care for the people who are reached, adequately provide ministry to members of all age groups, all the while, being ingenious with its finances, which are subject to weekly economic and emotional fluctuations of the congregation.

If *The Seven Laws* work for a church, they will certainly work for your business, your practice or your family.

TAKE THE MYSTERY OUT OF INCREASE.

As a young minister, I asked many seasoned pastors how to produce increase in my church.

I was given the usual rhetoric: "It takes a revival," or "It's God's Sovereignty that will grow your church. *You can't explain it."*

I pursued answers from pastors who seemingly had growing churches. I couldn't understand why they wouldn't answer my simple questions.

"How did you grow?"

"How did you build excitement?"

"How did you market your church?"

Their pat answers frustrated me.

So I prayed for revival. However, not having grown up in the Church, I honestly didn't know what revival would look like if it showed up. It seemed like a mystery.

I had heard about revivals. I had read how so many denominations were birthed out of revivals. I knew that they had a tremendous place in history, but I had no idea how you were selected by Sovereignty to receive one?

Then something astonishing happened. A revival *"broke out"* in a neighboring city. *(Even the terms people use to explain what happens when revival comes are mysterious.)*

WOW! Hundreds and thousands of people flocked into that city to experience the latest and greatest "revival." It was amazing.

What was also amazing was to see how the church that hosted the "revival" became a casualty to it. The local church turned into a "revival center" while long-standing members were crowded out. That church literally had thousands of people pouring in to it, yet very few of them stayed for the long haul.

"Is this how God truly builds the local church?" I wondered.

(Now, don't get me wrong—I appreciate and honor the Spirit of God—and the conversions were amazing.)

But then I thought, "If a revival like this showed up, what would I have to do to manage the people?"

This is where the church in the neighboring city had missed it. The increase was phenomenal, but they couldn't maintain it. They didn't have *The Seven Laws Which Govern Increase And Order* operating in their local body. To them their growth was a mystery. It came and it went.

On the other hand, I used to teach only *The Seven Laws,* but then I realized that you could practice all the laws that I teach and still not grow. You must have the eighth principle operating in your endeavors—which is *Grace To Grow.*

Grace to grow is what people often refer to as "revival." It's a supernatural flow of momentum that captures the hearts of people. It's an excitement—an enthusiasm—that is not easily explained. It is a charismatic experience that harmoniously draws the spirits of men.

After what I witnessed in that neighboring community, I began to study churches, businesses and organizations that had experienced increase and were able to maintain it. I searched out the largest churches in the world to find the common denominators which made them great.

_____ 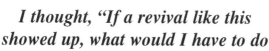 _____

I thought, "If a revival like this showed up, what would I have to do to manage the people.

_____ 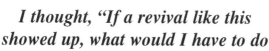 _____

I began to see principles from Scripture that these churches held as policies and philosophies of ministry. Each church I studied shared common threads of ministry, held common mentalities, and had similar organizational principles—even if they didn't know it.

But studying mega-churches is not necessarily the best way to grow a church. There are things mega-churches do that a church of 200, 300, or even 500 people can't do.

I attended one of the most influential pastor's conferences several years in a row hoping to gain instruction as to how to build a church. Each time I attended the conference I left inspired to believe God for greater things in my life and ministry. However, soon the inspiration evaporated like perspiration in a desert. Frustration replaced my excitement. Although I was *inspired,* I was not *instructed* to know the principles that would release increase in my church.

Holy frustration began to lead me to godly wisdom. Surprisingly it was found in the little things that I could do. I found simple applicable truths I could implement, which began to work. I began to experience personal and corporate growth. I then gravitated toward ministries and churches that shared my philosophy of practicality.

I conducted an exhaustive study on the twenty largest churches at that time and discovered they all shared common principles. Even though they differed in doctrine—no matter what their particular denominational affiliation or lack thereof—they shared a few absolute principles that governed their existence.

Half of those churches I studied would not make the top twenty today. Others, who have operated more efficiently, effectively and evangelistically, have surpassed them.

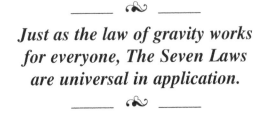

*Just as the law of gravity works
for everyone, The Seven Laws
are universal in application.*

About the same time as my inquiry, John Maxwell began to impact the church and business world with his laws on leadership. John has had a tremendous influence directing leaders to practice the laws of increase. His practical teachings have impacted me in numerous ways, as well.

Ultimately, the principles of *The Seven Laws Which Govern Increase And Order* are a result of discovering that the Bible says a lot about increase and how to maintain order.

Please understand that though I have personally used these truths in the arena of ministry, *The Seven Laws* are applicable to you. **Just as the law of gravity works for**

everyone, *The Seven Laws Of Increase And Order* **are universal in application.** The Bible says that the rain falls on the just and the unjust. If we work Biblical laws (or if we fail to work them), we enjoy (or suffer) the consequences.

When I was conducting my research, one of the fastest growing churches in America was a mega-church located in Oklahoma. One day as I was praying, I heard the Holy Spirit say in my heart, *"In ten days, the pastor of that church will call you."*

I had only briefly met this pastor a few times. He didn't really know me very well, so he had no reason to call.

Nevertheless, it came to pass just as the Holy Spirit said. Ten days later, the pastor called my cell phone and asked me to come serve on his staff as his Executive Pastor. Though few, the years I spent there proved invaluable to me. I enjoyed every minute of the opportunity to see, firsthand, the laws of increase and order put into practice.

The most valuable time for me while serving that congregation was the time spent in the department-head-level meetings. I saw the wisdom of God and the supernatural leading of the Holy Spirit present in the counsel of many. I still reflect on those meetings as special times.

When I left there to start a church in Orlando, Florida, I was distinctly impressed to apply *The Law Of Mutual Benefit* to my ministry. While I was starting the church, I was also led to travel and teach *The Seven Laws* to other churches, sharing with pastors and church leadership the unique opportunities and challenges that I have experienced pioneering two churches and serving on staff at a mega-church. Since that time, I have spoken at hundreds of churches, seminars and conferences teaching these principles.

I am always thrilled when I hear a praise report of what this teaching has done in a local church; however, I also hear good reports of how these principles have brought about increase in the lives of doctors, lawyers, business professionals, and housewives.

A professional entertainer recently shared with me that he teaches *The Seven Laws* to his family to help manage their home. A lawyer told me he applied these laws and tripled his practice. A doctor used them as the basis for the business plan for his new clinic. Now he has two locations, several associates and hundreds of patients. A single mother told me that she is teaching her son *The Seven Laws* to strengthen him spiritually and build his confidence as a young man.

What can the *Seven Laws* do for you?

They can help you achieve your goals, fulfill your dreams and accomplish your destiny. They can take you from mediocrity to excellence. They can raise you to a new standard of living. They can help your marriage, your finances and your peace of mind. They can give you direction on how to raise your children. I am convinced that *The Seven Laws Which Govern Increase And Order* work because they are Scriptural principles, and I have seen the results in hundreds of lives.

The motivation to see increase in life is not new. *To covet* means *to want what another person has at their expense.* But *to be blessed* means *to motivate others to desire your achievements.* There is nothing wrong with desiring increase. It is wrong only when we want increase at another's expense rather than paying the price for it ourselves.

I'll ask you again...

Have you realized that it's God's good pleasure to see success and increase in your life?

If so...

Are you willing to practice the principles He established in the Bible which govern divine increase and order?

Our search for increase and order begins in the beginning. God established the principle of increase with the first statement He ever made over man. *"Be fruitful and multiply!"*

Do you know that God has blessed you to increase?

Do you realize that it's God's will that you succeed?

You cannot succeed without a successor. God's idea of success includes reproduction, increase and multiplication.

God established *The First Law Of Increase* through the reproductive key that unlocks multiplication—**the seed**.

1 The Law Of Seed

Then God said, "Let the land produce vegetation: seed-bearing plants and trees on the land that bear fruit with seed in it, according to their various kinds." And it was so. The land produced vegetation: plants bearing seed according to their kinds and trees bearing fruit with seed in it according to their kinds. And God saw that it was good. And there was evening, and there was morning—the third day.   Genesis 1:11-13

Notice in the above passage the repeated phrase, *"according to their kinds."* **The first principle of *The Law Of Seed* is that seed must produce after its own kind.** Seed cannot choose to be different. Corn seed cannot say, "I'm tired of being corny." Corn seed must produce what it is—corn.

A friend visited a well-known teacher of the Word at his home. When he landed his private plane on the teacher's farm in Arkansas, he got out of the plane, looked around, and made an observation. "I see that you planted wheat this year. Last year, you didn't."

The teacher didn't reply.

Puzzled, the friend asked the teacher, "So, why did you plant wheat?"

The teacher smiled and answered simply, "Because I *wanted* wheat."

God created all seed with its own genetic code or pre-programming to determine and to produce fruit after its own kind.

Not long ago, my family and I enjoyed the movie, *"Second-Hand Lions."* One scene of the movie perfectly captures the principle of seed.

In the movie, two wealthy, elderly gentlemen live their lives as reclusively as possible until a relative abandons their young nephew on their farm. The boy gradually begins to win the hearts of the older men and brings a great deal of change to their lives.

In one scene of the movie, the uncles refuse to allow one traveling salesman after another the opportunity to share their sales pitches with them. One day, the boy questions their reasons for doing so. After a convincing argument from their nephew, the men finally give in and begin to listen to all the salesmen who come to their home. The uncles then begin buying anything and everything the salesmen have to offer.

One particular solicitor convinces the men that they should experience the joy of gardening. So the uncles purchase a variety of seed packets from him. They purchase all the proper clothing and tools for gardening. They read "How-To" books on growing vegetables. They even take great care to plant their seeds in neatly marked rows, expecting a harvest of beets, squash, tomatoes, potatoes, corn and onions. A few weeks later, their garden springs to life.

Unfortunately, as their garden begins to mature, the uncles and the boy realize they have an obvious problem. Every row they planted comes up corn. Even though each row was neatly titled something else, the harvest they received was all corn. The salesman was a con man, selling corn seed in different packages.

The gentlemen in the movie did everything right. They prepared the soil, planted the seed, watered the garden, and kept the weeds out. But the lesson they had to learn was: Seed will only produce what it is, no matter what you name it.

THE GIFT OF DOMINION

> *Now the earth was formless and empty, darkness was over the surface of the deep, and the Spirit of God was hovering over the waters.*
> *Genesis 1:2*

Here in this verse, the Bible tells us that the earth was formed out of chaos and emptiness. But we see a special creation process at work when God made man.

> *So God created man in his own image, in the image of God he created him; male and female he created them.*   *Genesis 1:27*

Only when God came to the point of creating man, did He make him in His own image and with His own likeness. This unique process establishes man and sets him apart from the rest of Creation. It positions man in a superior place, above everything else that was made. It gives man dominion and position. And along with that position comes authority. *(I'll talk more about authority later.)*

> *The creation waits in eager expectation for the sons of God to be revealed. For the creation was subjected to frustration, not by its own choice, but by the will of the one who subjected it, in hope that the creation itself will be liberated from its bondage*

> *to decay and brought into the glorious freedom of*
> *the children of God.*   Romans 8:19-21

From this passage, we must understand that leadership requires servanthood. The earth is servant to man, and man is servant to God. Other translations of the Scriptures confirm this, just as the NIV says, *Creation was subjected to frustration by the will of the one who subjected it.* Furthermore, the earth is waiting eagerly for the children of God to be revealed, when it will be liberated from the bonds of decay.

So man and earth are in a mutual-benefit relationship. Man benefits from the earth as long as he fulfills his responsibility of leadership. The earth suffers when man is disobedient to God's laws and is irresponsible concerning his duty as Servant-Leader.

Unfortunately, Adam did not take his place of dominion as God intended. The earth is now experiencing decay. It suffers from the violence of sin. As John Maxwell says, **"Everything rises and falls on leadership."**

> *God blessed them and said to them, "Be fruitful*
> *and increase in number; fill the earth and subdue it.*
> *Rule over the fish of the sea and the birds of the air*
> *and over every living creature that moves on the*
> *ground."*   Genesis 1:28

With this statement God gives man the position of dominion. This position is a gift from Creator God. God places man in the position of a steward who is responsible—that is, answerable to God—for his care and concern for God's creation.

We must walk in the dominion, or authority, that God gives to man. The gift of dominion is extremely valuable and establishes mankind in leadership.

You are in a position of leadership.

You must take your rightful place of authority over your life. *The Law Of Seed* is in your hand. But you must use it. You must plant the seed in order to reap a harvest.

God speaks a blessing over the male and female. He says, "Be fruitful and increase." He tells them to make fruit happen and to become great. He tells them how to enlarge, and how to become numerous.

YOU DETERMINE YOUR OWN DIET.

God always gives provision when He gives vision. This principle is revealed in the next statement of blessing.

> *Then God said, "I give you every seed-bearing plant on the face of the whole earth and every tree that has fruit with seed in it. They will be yours for food."*   Genesis 1:29

God transfers seed into the hands of man. It is man's responsibility to steward that seed.

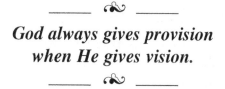

God always gives provision when He gives vision.

It is God's gift to man to determine his own diet. No other species on earth has the privilege that man has in this area. We are the only species who can satisfy our cravings by sowing and reaping.

What did you eat for breakfast this morning?

You had to ask yourself, "What do I want, and what choices do I have?"

You had to make a decision.

We have so many choices today that families argue over their decisions at most mealtimes. To make matters worse, Americans have mastered the art of fast food, so now we have more choices than ever.

With freedom comes responsibility. With choice comes consequence.

> *Do not be deceived: God cannot be mocked. A*
> *man reaps what he sows.*   *Galatians 6:7*

We have decisions to make in every area of life. God has ordained the principle of sowing and reaping to work in every realm. The principle of seed is universal in nature. It doesn't just apply to farming. It is applicable to life.

Paul applied the Old Testament commandment of "not muzzling the ox that is treading out the grain" to ministers who teach the Word, receiving financial support from their teaching (Deuteronomy 25:4, I Timothy 5:18). Paul's argument claims that ministers who are working *in the harvest* should receive their support and means of livelihood *from the harvest.*

In the same way, God gives us seed to plant in order that we may be partakers of the harvest produced by that seed.

BEGIN WITH THE BEGINNING.

Now let's look at another profile of creation to see another facet of *The Law Of Seed.*

> *In the beginning was the Word, and the Word was*
> *with God, and the Word was God. He was with*
> *God in the beginning. Through him all things were*
> *made; without him nothing was made that has been*
> *made.*   *John 1:1-3*

From this passage, we know that God spoke His Word, and the physical creation came into being from the reality of His thoughts. The God who calls those things that are not as though they are created everything by speaking. The source of all that we see is the spoken Word of God that came out from the Father. All things can *and will* pass away, but the Word of God cannot *and will not* return void.

This principle teaches me that if I am going to begin anything, I must begin with the Word of God.

The process of salvation works by this principle. You are saved when you believe in your heart that Jesus is Lord and He was raised from the dead, and when you confess that belief with your tongue. It is with the heart that you believe and with the tongue that you confess (Romans 10:9-10). When you speak your belief—when you confess it—you become a new creation. *"Old things have passed away; behold, all things are become new"* (II Corinthians 5:17 KJV).

Proverbs 18:21 tells us, *"The tongue has the power of life and death."* It is through your expressed words of faith that life begins.

Let this next principle sink in to your heart:

If *ANY* of your words matter, then *ALL* of your words matter.

If Jesus said to you, "You will have *everything* that you say with your mouth," wouldn't you be more careful to watch what you said?

YOU ARE A CREATIONIST.

"The God who made the world and everything in it is the Lord of heaven and earth and does not live in temples built by hands. And he is not served by human hands, as if he needed anything, because he himself gives all men life and breath and everything else. From one man he made every nation of men, that they should inhabit the whole earth; and he

determined the times set for them and the exact
places where they should live...."

Acts 17:24-26

Most Christians live an evolutionary lifestyle even though they do not believe in the Theory. They think that someday their lives are going to evolve into bliss. They expect that they will awaken one day to find that their lives have suddenly become perfect.

Of course this will never happen. You cannot wake up in a bed that is already made. You have to get up every morning and make the bed yourself.

The Evolutionist does not think in terms of purposes, plans and pursuits. He thinks in terms of accidents, luck and fate. For him, life is chaotic—a series of accidental and uncontrollable events. The byproduct of this thinking is situational ethics. His life lacks purpose.

As a believer, you cannot afford to allow this kind of thinking to influence you. You must think as a Creationist thinks.

Understanding the principle of seed in Scripture defeats the Theory of Evolution.

You must ask yourself: "Where do I begin? What is my purpose? My destiny? God's will?"

Myles Munroe says, *"Where the purpose is unknown, abuse is inevitable."*

If you do not know your purpose, you will never take your place at God's table. If a husband doesn't understand the purpose of marriage, he will abuse his wife. If a father doesn't understand the purpose of parenthood, he will abuse his children. If a man or woman doesn't understand the purpose of sexual relations, his or her life will be filled with abuse, unfulfillment and dissatisfaction.

For an example, if we do not understand the God-given purpose of grain, we will pervert it from the nutritional substance of bread, and manipulate it to become the destructive force of alcohol. The substance that gives life can also take life. The entire illegal drug epidemic today is caused by the misuse of vegetation.

To think like a Creationist, you must realize that all things in Creation have their purpose and source in the Word of God. The source of all beginnings is God's Word. Nothing is made, which has been made, without Him.

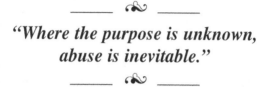

"Where the purpose is unknown, abuse is inevitable."

When my wife, Kay, and I became engaged, I had to learn to begin our lives with the Word. I didn't know how to be a husband. My mother and father divorced when I was a baby. My stepfather did not model what a good husband should be, so I turned to the Word of God for answers.

To begin my marriage as God purposed for it to be, I began with the Word. I learned that to be a good husband means you must become frugal and skilled in the management of cultivation. *(To cultivate means to prepare soil for growing crops; to improve or to develop something;* or *to develop an acquaintance or intimacy with someone.)*

I found out that I have to learn how to "farm," if I'm going to be a good husband. (The word *husband* comes from the term *husbandry,* which literally means *the science, skill or art of farming;* or *the frugal and sensible management of resources.)* In other words, I must cultivate my wife.

I learned that my wife is a reflection of my skill as a farmer. I plant seeds—*my words*—within her, and harvest fruits—*the results*—from her (Ephesians 5:24-27). I plant, she incubates, and I harvest. If I don't like what I'm looking at after a season of time, it's my own fault. It's my responsibility as a husband to cultivate my wife.

When God placed Adam in Eden, He gave him the gift of seed. God made Adam a gardener. It's important to notice that God didn't make the entire earth a garden. Outside the Garden of Eden was untapped and untamed potential. The Garden was just a start. That's the way God operates. He gives us a start. He gives us seed. Then He points us to our destiny of dreams.

"Go increase and be fruitful," He says to us.

> *Now he who supplies seed to the sower and bread for food will also supply and increase your store of seed and will enlarge the harvest of your righteousness.*   II Corinthians 9:10

God will supply you with seed. You can't plant seed unless you first have received it. God will always give you a gift of seed when He gives you opportunity to increase.

A seed thought can incubate within you to become an idea. The idea can become an income. God doesn't just rain down money on you from the sky. God's currency is wisdom, knowledge, favor, insight, understanding, witty inventions and creativity. These are the things God gives you as seed to bring you increase.

GOD'S WAYS ARE SUPERIOR TO OURS.

Jesus explained the ways of God's kingdom through the teaching of parables. He revealed the mysteries of the ages through practical teachings—though sometimes misunderstanding may cloud the hearer. The disciples failed to understand many things. They asked Jesus about the meaning of His parables. He responded by saying:

> *He said, "The knowledge of the secrets of the kingdom of God has been given to you, but to others I speak in parables, so that, 'though seeing, they may not see; though hearing, they may not understand.'"*   *Luke 8:10*

This is amazing. Jesus said that the parables reveal the secrets of God's kingdom. *(When I first read this I wanted to go back and read all the parables! I wanted to understand God's secrets.)*

According to Colossians 1:25-28, God's mysteries are to be revealed to us at this time. If we can understand God's way of doing something, we can do it His way.

> *He made known his ways to Moses, his deeds to the people of Israel.*   *Psalms 103:7*

Believe me, when you know God's *ways,* you are superior to those who have only experienced his *deeds.* The 5,000 who were feed by Jesus followed him searching for more signs—more acts. Their hunger was fixed upon temporary relief and satisfaction. What they failed to recognize was that He wanted to show them *His ways* of supply.

Let me explain this with the principle of healing. There are two types of healing provided for in the atonement of Christ. One is through what is called the Gifts of Healings (I Corinthians 12:9, 28). The Gifts of Healings are simply that. They are supernatural gifts from the Holy Spirit.

There are those who receive these manifestations of the Holy Spirit in a church service or in a crusade, and they are miraculously healed. Yet sometimes, their sickness may return days, weeks or months later.

Why does this happen?

It happens because the person who battled the sickness
didn't receive understanding and instruction to sustain their
healing. They may have returned to their old way of
thinking, speaking and living. They may have returned to
their poor diet or their way of life that allowed sickness to
come in in the first place.

The second way to receive bodily healing is by faith. Faith
comes by hearing the Word of God (Romans 10:17). When
you plant the seed of God's Word concerning healing in
your heart, by hearing it and accepting it, the fruit of that
seed is healing.

This manner of healing will last a lifetime because you
know the source of healing. Life is in the Word. The Word
renews your mind and gives you the thought processes of
Christ. *"We have the mind of Christ"* (I Corinthians 2:16).

THE SEED IS THE WORD OF GOD.

The parable of the farmer who sowed seed reveals how the
Word of God works in our lives. The seed is the Word of
God (Luke 8:11, Mark 4:16).

In reality, each seed is a mini-testimonial whenever a
farmer plants it. Every seed testifies of God's creation. It
testifies of God's principle of increase. It testifies of God's
precision and order. It also testifies of God's provision.

In the parable of the sower, four types of soil are described:
the path, the rocky places, the thorn-infested ground and the
good soil. The first three soil recipients shed light on why
the seed *doesn't* work. The fourth soil illustrates how it
does. *(It's as important to know what causes seed not to
work, as it is to find out why it does work.)*

THE PATH

> *"Some people are like seed along the path, where
> the word is sown. As soon as they hear it, Satan*

comes and takes away the word that was sown in them."

Mark 4:15

The path, or way side, represents the hardened heart. When people live in sin, their hearts become calloused by the pain, troubles and hurts of life. You see it on their faces. Weathered looks, wrinkled brows, dimmed eyes, all show outward signs of their difficulties. When the Word is sown in hardened hearts, satan comes and takes it away. The seed cannot penetrate here.

The Bible says that God's goodness leads us to repentance, but because of stubbornness and unrepentant hearts, people store up wrath unto themselves (Romans 2:4-5).

When you read the Word of God, it can only penetrate the pliable areas of your life. If you harbor bitterness, resentment, unforgiveness or anger, the Word cannot be received. Satan is constantly bringing situations into our lives to gain a foothold.

Growing up in Oklahoma, I learned the principle of the path from watching our cattle make their daily trip to the barn. Cattle are funny. They have fields to wander in and enjoy, but when it comes to traveling, they like paths. When they travel in their herds, they normally get in line and follow the leader. They hope the leader knows where he's going and they follow right behind him. Their view doesn't change much. As they travel, they pound out a path. Nothing can grow in that path.

In much the same way, the man with the hardened heart is so road weary that he seldom receives anything new. His world is only as big as the trails that he drives. His motto is, "I've never done it that way before."

Few people ever wander off their chosen paths in life. In fact, archeologists today can discover the habits of ancient peoples when they uncover their trails of long ago.

When the seed of the Word is sown in your heart, satan comes immediately to steal it. The devil fears the seed. He knows that if the seed of the Word can get into the protective arena of your heart, your life can change.

If you are going to harvest fruit and enjoy increase, you must rid yourself of hardness of heart. You must plow up the dry, crusty ground in order for the seed of God's Word to be planted in you.

What bitter root is holding you back?

Do you have unforgiveness in your heart?

Have you allowed stubbornness to keep you from receiving your harvest?

Remember, it is the kindness of God that leads you to repentance. When you repent you become pliable, usable and possible. Potential is returned to your life.

THE STONY PLACES

> *"Others, like seed sown on rocky places, hear the word and at once receive it with joy. But since they have no root, they last only a short time. When trouble or persecution comes because of the word, they quickly fall away."*   Mark 4:16-17

The second kind of soil recipient is the rocky places. When seed is sown in a stony field it is received at first. But because the seed can't take hold, it can't stand the test of trials.

Jesus said whenever the Word is sown, immediately trouble and persecution will come.

When I accepted Jesus as my Savior I was so happy. My life had been filled with pain. I had been overwhelmed with trouble. My young dreams had been shattered. Trusted people disappointed me. Immediately after I made the decision for salvation, I was laid off my job. I couldn't believe it. I thought, "Why should I loose my job three days after I accepted the Lord? Isn't this supposed to be the time for me to begin to enjoy the blessings of God?"

All these things were an attempt to derail me before I could gain momentum. It was satan's endeavor to crush my spirit and to abort my salvation.

Understand this: The devil always attacks infancy.

The Bible tells us that the devil is like a lion, roaming the earth seeking whom he may devour (I Peter 5:8). Satan attacks the weak, the infant and the crippled.

Satan will always go after the Word in its infancy. He knows that the seed has the potential to bring deliverance.

He possessed Pharaoh and caused him to fear the sons of Israel, so Pharaoh ordered all the baby boys to be killed. Satan feared the deliverer—but Moses was a special child, and his mother hid him.

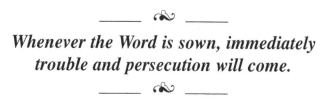

Whenever the Word is sown, immediately trouble and persecution will come.

At the time of Jesus' birth, the heavens declared His coming. Satan feared the Promised Child, so he persuaded Herod to kill all the boys who were two-years old and under in the vicinity of Jerusalem. Only because of God's divine protection, the Messiah escaped.

Notice that the stony ground represents trouble and persecution. As soon as you receive the Word, satan manipulates people to turn on you, to intimidate you or to crush you with pressure.

It's in the rocky places that the seed can't get deep enough to take root. Rocky people are shallow people. They get so excited the minute they hear the Word, yet they lack the ability to let the Word dig in deep. They will often repeat Scriptural truths with you, but they won't apply them to their own lives.

As a minister, it is my responsibility to preach the full counsel of God's Word. When I am led to preach a certain truth from the Bible, it seems I am usually challenged in that very truth. It is the devil's attempt to intimidate me and keep me from preaching God's Word.

If I preach on healing, either my family or I will usually be attacked with sickness. If I preach on God's Word concerning finances, satan will try to attack my finances. At first, I used to take this personally, but then I realized, it's just business. Satan attacks the Word. When he does, I simply return the Word, which rebukes him and stops his fiery attacks of doubt and unbelief (Ephesians 6:16).

Most people will not put their faith in God's Word above their personal experiences. This is a shallow way of living. King Solomon struggled throughout the Book of Ecclesiastes with the vanities of life, because his explorations of experience did not reveal wisdom. He concluded that obedience to God's Word is the meaning and purpose of existence.

THE PLACE OF THORNS

> *"Still others, like seed sown among thorns, hear the word; but the worries of this life, the deceitfulness of wealth and the desires for other things come in and choke the word, making it unfruitful."*
> *Mark 4:18-19*

The third type of soil described in the parable of the sower is the place of thorns. Jesus said that there are those who hear the Word, but the worries of life, the deceitfulness of riches and the desires for other things choke out the Word.

If satan can't make you harden your heart, and if he can't intimidate you so the Word won't be allowed to take root, he will try to distract you.

This type of attack reaches deep within an individual. The Word is heard, but worries and fears begin to suffocate it.

To worry literally means *to be drawn in different directions.* Satan knows that a double-minded man is unstable. Therefore, his scheme is to bombard you with thoughts of fear and doubt. He gets desperate because of the Word.

I have seen this in my own life. The ministry is filled with constant distractions.

When I first developed the habit of prayer, I was amazed at how distracted my mind could become. As soon as I would start down a path of prayer, I would think of everything I needed to do that day. When I would pull my mind back on track, the phone would ring, or someone would interrupt me. I learned to get up early in the morning to pray and to take a note pad with me to write down the things I needed to do. I also learned to find a place of seclusion to pray. Jesus often withdrew from the multitude and from His own team to pray (Luke 5:16).

The sad reality about the thorny place is that these are good people. They receive the Word, but because of distractions they can't receive from God.

Riches can distract and deceive many people. The deceitfulness of riches robs them of the true wealth that God promises the believer.

Most people are in the constant pursuit of money. Don't make this mistake. The Word says you are to seek the kingdom first—then the things of life will be added to you

(Matthew 6:33). *Provision is a byproduct of seeking wisdom.* Wisdom is the principal thing (Proverbs 4:7).

Now, don't go to the other extreme by thinking that poverty equals holiness. Many people are trapped in the "poverty mentality." For hundreds of years, Christians have claimed that holiness and poverty walk hand in hand. You must have balance. Solomon said that the man who fears God will avoid all extremes (Ecclesiastes 7:18).

My heart has hurt for people so many times when I've seen them become arrogant because of the deceitfulness of riches. They become haughty and self righteous, thinking that because they have material wealth, they're spiritually superior to others. Their offerings become bribes. If they don't get their way, they become venomous. Because these people believe that their gain is godliness, the Word is choked out of their lives.

THE GOOD SOIL

> *"Others, like seed sown on good soil, hear the word, accept it, and produce a crop—thirty, sixty or even a hundred times what was sown."*
>   *Mark 4:20*

The forth recipient of the seed in the parable is the good soil. You want to be good soil. When you receive God's Word and accept it, then you produce. In fact, you produce multiplied times over the original plant.

I am amazed at how many times I can receive new insight or revelation from a scripture that I've read before. When I hear a message on a subject that I've heard a hundred times, I can receive a new truth, a new application or new insight into God's way of doing things.

That's how *The Law Of Seed* works. When you receive the seed, the seed's potential is released. You learn the character of God by hearing about His ways.

You see, every seed has a protective coating. This covering locks in the potency of life. The only way the protective coating of the Word can be penetrated is by faith. We must not only hear the Word, but we must receive it, mixing it with faith (Hebrews 4:2).

> *So then faith cometh by hearing, and hearing by the word of God.*   Romans 10:17 KJV

As you receive from God's Word, you enlarge your capacity to receive more faith and more seed.

A young boy had a huge puff of cotton candy in his hand when his dad asked, "How can a small boy eat so much cotton candy?"

The boy replied, "Maybe I'm bigger on the inside than I am on the outside."

As you receive from God's Word, you enlarge your capacity to receive more faith and more seed.

The protective coating on a seed allows it to last for ages. Modern archeologists have discovered seeds dating back to early civilizations, which when planted in good soil and tended to properly, still spring to life.

The Seed that God sows is incorruptible seed. Those who receive the Word of God are given the power to become children of God (John 1:12).

> *For you have been born again, not of perishable seed, but of imperishable, through the living and enduring word of God.*   I Peter 1:23

The Greek word for *imperishable* is derived from the first letter in the Greek alphabet, symbolizing that the first letter or numeral is incorruptible. Jesus Christ is the Word of God. He is the beginning—the Alpha. The Word of God will stand forever.

> *"As the heavens are higher than the earth, so are my ways higher than your ways and my thoughts than your thoughts. As the rain and the snow come down from heaven, and do not return to it without watering the earth and making it bud and flourish, so that it yields seed for the sower and bread for the eater, so is my word that goes out from my mouth: It will not return to me empty, but will accomplish what I desire and achieve the purpose for which I sent it."* Isaiah 55:9-11

As you sow God's Word, you will find that seed does not return void. Within the Word is the potential of life, purpose and achievement.

_____ ⟋ _____

POINTS FOR INCREASE:

Seed must produce after it's own kind.

You have been given dominion in life.

You determine your own diet.

All things begin with the Word.

We are Creationists.

God's ways are superior to ours.

The seed is the Word.

_____ ⟋ _____

2 The Law Of Attraction

"For everyone who has will be given more, and he will have an abundance. Whoever does not have, even what he has will be taken from him."
                                        Matthew 25:29

In the parable of the talents, Jesus reveals an amazing principle that I call *The Law Of Attraction.*

We attract more of whatever we prove to be faithful in.

"Again, it will be like a man going on a journey, who called his servants and entrusted his property to them. To one he gave five talents of money, to another two talents, and to another one talent, each according to his ability. Then he went on his journey."   *Matthew 25:14-15*

Jesus tells His disciples a story of a man who was leaving for an extended trip. Wisely, the man wanted his money to work for him while he was away.

Jesus said that the boss called three of his managers in to give them instructions for managing his wealth while he was gone. To the first manager, the man gave five talents. *(A talent was worth more than a thousand dollars at that time, so to make this easy to relate to, we'll say the first manager was given more than five thousand dollars to invest, and so on.)*

To the second manager, the man entrusted two talents— more than two thousand dollars.

Finally, the third manager received just over a thousand.

Jesus points out that since the boss employed all three managers and had opportunity to watch them work on a regular basis, the man already knew the abilities, or skill levels, of each of the three men.

GOD INVESTS IN PROVEN ABILITIES.

Have you noticed yourself seemingly hitting the ceiling of success?

Does it seem as if you just can't get the break, the promotion, the bonus or the commission you dream of?

I must admit, I've felt that way in my life from time to time.

But then I learned the secret of *The Law Of Attraction.*

That is, if I am going to experience increase, I must master *faithfulness in the least.*

The principle of tithing is a great example of how *The Law Of Attraction* works.

God has promised us in His Word that our tithes open the windows of Heaven (Malachi 3:10). Yet few people really believe this truth. They go down the road of life, offering different arguments such as: why they don't have to tithe, or why they can't afford to tithe, or whatever. No matter what they say, the simple truth is this: *They don't believe God's Word.*

God said in His Word that when you pay your tithes, He provides you with a guarantee that He will pour divinely-appointed blessings into your life.

I hear people say all the time, "The tithe is ten percent of your increase."

That sounds simple enough. Right?

But wait...

The tithe is *the first* ten percent.

The first ten percent is the part that is *the redemptive portion,* not the second or the last. In Genesis, Abel's offering received favor because it was the *first* portion. Cain's offering did not receive favor because it was *"some"* of the fruit.

Tithing means that you are giving the *first* ten percent of your increase. When you practice tithing, the tithe acts as a key to the chambers of Heaven's treasuries. God's divine currencies of ideas, insights, favor, open doors, wisdom and new concepts become open to you. Therefore, each time you receive finances, the tithe gives you an opportunity to be promoted to the next level in life.

It's your choice.

God doesn't have to make a decision concerning His blessing for your life; you choose or reject His blessing by what you do with His Word. If you are faithful in the few—or the least—God has promised that you will attract more in your life.

I heard a story once about a young businessman who approached the late Pastor John Osteen of Lakewood Church in Houston, Texas, years ago. He asked Pastor Osteen to pray with him about a new business that he had started.

The young man made a vow to the pastor saying, "I will give ten percent of everything that my new company makes to the Lord."

Pastor Osteen prayed a prayer of agreement with the young entrepreneur.

As the business grew, the tithes from the company increased dramatically.

Later, the then-successful businessman returned to Pastor Osteen. "I've been faithful to tithe off my business all this time, but now it's really a lot of money, at thousands of dollars each week," He said. "Is there any way I can get out of my vow?"

Pastor Osteen smiled and replied, "Well, I can pray with you that your company will start to loose money so that you can afford to tithe again."

The businessman exclaimed, "No, no, Pastor. I get the point!"

YOU MUST BE FAITHFUL IN THE FEW.

"The man who had received the five talents went at once and put his money to work and gained five more. So also, the one with the two talents gained two more. But the man who had received the one talent went off, dug a hole in the ground and hid his master's money. After a long time the master of those servants returned and settled accounts with them. The man who had received the five talents brought the other five. 'Master,' he said, 'you entrusted me with five talents. See, I have gained five more.' His master replied, 'Well done, good and faithful servant! You have been faithful with a few things; I will put you in charge of many things. Come and share your master's happiness!' The man with the two talents also came. 'Master,' he said, 'you entrusted me with two talents; see, I have gained two more.' His master replied, 'Well done, good and faithful servant! You have been faithful

*with a few things; I will put you in charge of many
things. Come and share your master's happiness!'"*
                                        Matthew 25:16-23

While the man in Jesus' parable was on his trip, the
faithfulness of his managers was revealed.

After he returned, the boss called the first manager in for an
audit. The employee with five thousand dollars
experienced a 200% return.

"Good job!" said his boss. "You've proven yourself to me.
I want you to enjoy yourself and become my partner."

The second manager also reported a 200% return.

"Good job!" said the boss. "Enjoy yourself and I will
promote you."

_____ ◌◌ _____

Faithfulness (or the lack of it) attracts (or repels) promotion.

_____ ◌◌ _____

By being faithful, both the first and the second manager
doubled their ability!

The Law Of Attraction states that whenever you've proven
yourself to be faithful in one level, you are then positioned
for promotion.

Notice that the boss did not invest in their *talents;* he
invested his talents in their *character.* In other words,
faithfulness is the character trait that a master is looking for
in his stewards—not just special gifting. Faithfulness (or
the lack of it) attracts (or repels) promotion.

> *"Then the man who had received the one talent
> came. 'Master,' he said, 'I knew that you are a
> hard man, harvesting where you have not sown and*

*gathering where you have not scattered seed. So I
was afraid and went out and hid your talent in the
ground. See, here is what belongs to you.' His
master replied, 'You wicked, lazy servant! So you
knew that I harvest where I have not sown and
gather where I have not scattered seed? Well then,
you should have put my money on deposit with the
bankers, so that when I returned I would have
received it back with interest. Take the talent from
him and give it to the one who has the ten talents.'
For everyone who has will be given more, and he
will have an abundance. Whoever does not have,
even what he has will be taken from him."*

Matthew 25:24-29

The third manager who was given one talent, or one
thousand dollars, said, "Sir, I knew your standards were
extreme and you were very demanding and hard. I was
intimidated by you, so I took your money and secured it in
a good hiding place so I wouldn't loose it. Here's the full
amount back."

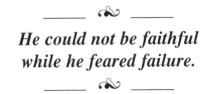

*He could not be faithful
while he feared failure.*

The boss got mad and said, "You knew this wouldn't cut it
with me. You knew my standards and that I expect the best
in everything. Yet, you did the very least! Why didn't you
deposit my money in the bank? They would have at least
given you a little interest."

The attitude of the third employee was terrible. It's what
limited his ability. He could not be faithful while he feared
failure.

The boss entrusted his money to this employee—that means he believed in him enough to invest in him—yet, this employee didn't believe in his boss.

You will never be able to take a risk for greater reward when you live in fear.

If you fear failure, you will not succeed. Furthermore, if you haven't failed at anything, you haven't tried anything. The greater the reward—the greater the risk.

The great scientist and genius Albert Einstein once said, "Nothing of great value has ever been achieved without facing violent opposition."

OPERATE *NOW* WHAT YOU'D BE FORCED TO OPERATE *WHEN....*

To practice *The Law Of Attraction*, we must operate *now* what we would be forced to operate *when....*

Describe your dream.

Where do you see yourself a year—three years—or five years from now?

Stop!

What will you be forced to become or to do when you are there?

Will you have to have education? experience? knowledge? proficiency in an area that you don't have now?

Operate *now* what you will be forced to operate *when...* and you will have what you dreamed.

As I was planting our second church in Orlando, Florida, I began to strategize my expectation for our growth. I examined every area of our ministry. I took note that we did not have a class for preschool children.

I asked the minister in charge of the children, "How many preschoolers do we have in the church?"

He informed me that we had one preschooler and that they cared for him in the church nursery.

Right then and there, I realized that our church wouldn't grow until we followed the principle of *operating now what we would be forced to operate when* we had more preschoolers. We invested several thousand dollars to practice this principle. We recruited and trained workers. We got everything ready and opened a new class for our one preschooler.

Within *two weeks,* we grew to *eight preschoolers!*

A young man came up to me one night in church asking me to believe with him to find a job.

I assured him that God was in favor of his request, but before I prayed, I asked him what time he woke up every morning.

He responded, "Oh, I usually get up around 9:00 AM."

I challenged him and said, "People with jobs get up at 6:00 in the morning."

I told him that his job was to get a job. I shared that he should do *now* what he would be forced to do *when* he got a job.

The next week he came up to me with a praise report.

"I did what you told me," he said. "On Monday, I got up at 6:00 AM, and left the house to get a newspaper. While I was driving down the road, I saw a manufacturing plant. I felt impressed to pull in and to inquire if they had any jobs available. They hired me on the spot because one of their employees had slept in that morning."

This young man practiced this principle and got a new job. I learned this principle years ago by learning to be faithful with my automobiles.

When I attended Bible college, I sold my possessions to invest in my education and I was given an old Chevrolet Chevette to drive. Although it had very few miles on it, this car had been sitting unused for years. My brother-in-law tuned the motor up and got it running for me.

To be honest, it was humbling. That old car was not exactly what I wanted to be seen in, but I was grateful.

I worked in a car wash to make a living while attending college, so every day I would clean my car, wax it, treat the tires and spray "new car" fragrance inside. I had waxed it so much that the rust on the outside was the best-protected rust on any car you've ever seen.

One day, I took my car to get new tires. Apparently it was an amusing experience for the worker assigned to my car. He called all the other workers over to look at my old tires. I wondered what they were laughing about.

He told me, "On the outside these tires look brand new, and on the inside they have wires sticking out of them. You've been driving on nothing but Armor-All!"

At any rate, I was faithful to take care of that car. A year later, God blessed me with a new car.

DON'T DESPISE SMALL BEGINNINGS.

Most people have great dreams but they fail to achieve them because they despise small beginnings. You will never attract increase consistently in your life until you realize that it is in the small details of life where victory is won.

David was chosen to become the king of Israel after the Holy Spirit rejected King Saul and each of David's brothers

(I Samuel 16). The Bible says that from the day that Samuel anointed David to be king, the Holy Spirit came upon David in power (I Samuel 16:13).

Yet, what did David do after being anointed with the oil from Samuel's flask?

He returned to care for his father's sheep.

One day, David arrived at the battle line of the Israelites and the Philistines with supplies for his brothers. He overheard the threats of Goliath, the champion fighter from the Philistine camp. He also heard the promise of King Saul for the man who would take out the champion—the promise of great wealth, complete tax exemption and the king's daughter in marriage.

Disguised in this crisis was an opportunity.

Many times our greatest opportunities are found in crisis. The late President John F. Kennedy once said, "When written in Chinese, the word *crisis* is composed of two characters—one represents *danger*—the other represents *opportunity*."

You see, even though David had received the anointing to be the next king of Israel, he was not in the natural lineage for the throne. He was not Saul's natural son. But by killing the giant, David would step into his kingdom destiny. Marrying the king's daughter gave David a place in the natural lineage of royalty.

David's brother Eliab, who had been rejected by the Prophet Samuel, accused David of failing to care for *"those few sheep,"* and then slandered him by calling David arrogant when he said he could kill the giant.

David was not being arrogant, he simply was confident of victory because he'd already proven himself faithful in the small things. David had protected his *"few sheep"* from a lion and a bear. The giant was just his next step.

> *"The LORD who delivered me from the paw of the*
> *lion and the paw of the bear will deliver me from*
> *the hand of this Philistine." Saul said to David,*
> *"Go, and the LORD be with you."*
>
> *I Samuel 17:37*

When you prove yourself faithful in small steps, God promotes you to greater risks—and greater, potential rewards. God has confidence in you.

Here's another principle you can learn from *The Law Of Attraction:* **As long as you despise where you are now, you will never leave there.**

Understand that the place where you are now, is a temporary place. You are a nomad in the journey of ability. You don't want to settle down and set up camp in one place. You must master your current position in order to go further in life.

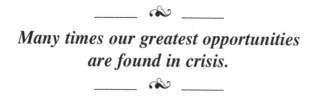

Many times our greatest opportunities
are found in crisis.

God rescued the people of Israel out of the bondage of slavery in Egypt through the leadership of Moses. Just three days after Pharaoh and his army perished in the sea, the Israelites arrived at Marah. They couldn't drink the water there because it was bitter, so the people grumbled against Moses (Exodus 15:22-24).

How quickly we forget the miracles of the past when we are suffering the discomfort of today. When we forget that God has blessed us and brought to the place where we are, we become ungrateful.

> *"I will increase the number of men and animals upon you, and they will be fruitful and become numerous. I will settle people on you as in the past and will make you prosper more than before. Then you will know that I am the LORD. I will cause people, my people Israel, to walk upon you. They will possess you, and you will be their inheritance...."*   *Ezekiel 36:11-12a*

This is a unique portion of scripture. God speaks a promise to the mountains of Israel and tells them that they would be teeming with life again after being uninhabited for so many years.

The King James Bible translates the last phrase in verse twelve as:

> *"...And thou shalt no more henceforth bereave them of men."*   *Ezekiel 36:12b*

But I believe the reason God speaks this promise to the mountains is better revealed from the New International translation, which says:

> *"...You will never again deprive them of their children."*   *Ezekiel 36:12b*

A society is known by the way it treats its children. God prophesies in Malachi that the land will be cursed, if the fathers do not turn their hearts toward their children (Malachi 4:6). This is the principle of despising small beginnings.

In order to justify abortion, many people in the world explain away these "small beginnings" by calling babies something other than what they are ("a fetus," "an embryo," etc.). But no matter what the world says, *children are children!*

We must not abort the seeds of our dreams—those tiny ideas and hopes in us which have the potential of greatness.

MAKE ROOM FOR INCREASE.

The Law Of Attraction demands that you must make room in your life for increase. As you plant your seed and water it, you must make room for it to grow.

Let me explain this principle by using your schedule.

In order to have increase in your life, you must make time for it. Time is a currency. We are all given 1,440 minutes in a day. You spend the currency of your time on many things or with many people.

How valuable is your time?

Here in the United States, we have a law which guarantees that a worker must be paid a minimum amount of money for an hourly wage. Minimum wage is not enough to live a comfortable life. It is just what the name implies—a minimum.

The only way a worker in this country can experience increase at minimum wage is by exchanging more of his time. He must work more hours to receive more money. On the other hand, there are those people here who are paid outrageous amounts of money for only a few seconds of their time.

Most people do not honestly know how much they are worth. Phone calls, television, traffic jams and waiting in lines all sap productivity out of them. The average person never realizes the true value of his time.

Jesus was different. He knew the value of His time. He understood His destiny.

In John 7:6, Jesus told His brothers, "The right time (or opportunity) for Me hasn't come yet. For you any time is right."

Jesus understood the timing for His life. He was unwilling to waste any of His time. He was being pressured to leave because the Jews were looking for an opportunity to kill him. He wouldn't give in to the pressure. He was in control of his destiny.

If you are going to experience increase in your life you must become aware of timing.

THE 50% TIME RULE

My goal is to operate on what I call *The 50% Time Rule.* In other words, I always try to keep 50% of my time available for increase.

Now, that doesn't mean that I work only half of the time. It means that half of my time is at my discretion. I have room to grow because I have made time for it. Even while I plant a church, or when I travel conducting seminars, conferences, and church services, I also write, relax, date my wife and enjoy my children.

I enjoy traveling and teaching *The Seven Laws Of Order And Increase.* I learned early on, however, that I would have to share my expectations for my schedule with the host churches where I was to be teaching.

After a few blunders, I realized that I was the best person to know what the seminar was tailored to accomplish and how best to accomplish it. When I began to organize my time with the people I travelled to minister to, everyone was happier. I was in control of my time, and they got the best seminar possible.

I even practice the principles of managing my time in the little things.

When I receive a phone call, I normally tell the caller in advance the amount of time that I have to speak with them. I have found that this forces conversations to come to the point and makes them more effective. When I place a phone call, I normally ask the person I'm calling for permission to speak to them for a certain length of time. Then I honor it.

As a pastor, people often expect my time to be at their disposal. Their thinking is based on the image of the old country parson who would visit his congregants each week, drinking coffee or tea at each stop.

I tried that early in my ministry and found myself with caffeine jitters every evening. I also realized that as the church grew, the people who built their relationships with me around coffee or tea did not value my teaching and preaching, and they soon left my church.

The highest form of relationship you can have with any minister is built around his ministry gift—not around his personality. His ministry gift will equip you and make you a better Christian (Ephesians 4:11-12). His personality may fail you. You may become too familiar with him if he is in your life too much, and then you will not benefit from his ministry.

Familiarity breeds contempt. Proverbs 25:17 says, "Seldom set foot in your neighbor's house—too much of you and he will hate you."

Another facet of *The Law Of Attraction* is that you must use it constantly in order to experience increase. When God gives you something new to accomplish, you still must be faithful to keep up with the things you were doing before, in order to continue to attract increase and step up to the next level that He has for you.

How do you do this?

It's not as difficult as it sounds.

I will explain it in detail in *Chapter 4, The Law Of Reflex* later on.

_____ ๛ _____

POINTS FOR INCREASE:

Be faithful in the few in order to attract more.

Understand that God invests in proven abilities.

*Operate now what you would be forced
to operate when....*

Do not despise small beginnings.

Make room for increase.

Operate on The 50% Time Rule.

_____ ๛ _____

3 The Law Of Hospitality

Offer hospitality to one another without grumbling.
Each one should use whatever gift he has received
to serve others, faithfully administering God's grace
in its various forms.   *I Peter 4:9-10*

The Law Of Hospitality is one of the greatest principles in
Scripture. It releases the Gifts of the Holy Spirit which
empower the Church to function as the supplier of the needs
of humanity.

Hospitality is defined as *the kind or generous treatment*
offered to guests or strangers. When a host is *hospitable,* it
means *he treats his guests as honored and valuable.*

When we practice hospitality, then grace, favor and
anointing are released into our lives.

I see *The Law Of Hospitality* at work whenever I travel.
When a host church has prepared for my arrival and really
put effort into their preparations, the Gifts of the Spirit
seemingly flow unabated.

However, when I arrive at a place that seems to be
tolerating, rather than celebrating my time with them, the
Gifts of the Spirit are hindered. Usually it is a waste of
time and effort.

Years ago, when I first learned of this principle, I practiced hospitality by giving honor to our missionaries whenever they were visiting my church in Mobile.

I recall the first time that I "rolled out the red carpet," so to speak, for a guest missionary.

When he and his family arrived, we had arranged for them to have two first-class hotel rooms, overlooking the beautiful Mobile Bay. *(The sunsets are spectacular there.)* We had prepared the room with gifts for each of the missionary's children, a gift for his wife and a nice tie for him to wear.

When that missionary stepped onto my pulpit, the anointing was so strong upon him that he was moved with emotion. He thanked my congregation for the overwhelming hospitality and then shared his vision for reaching the lost of the world.

After that single event, my mission's budget doubled at our church. That began to set a course for us to consciously practice *The Law Of Hospitality* for all of our guests.

I then turned my efforts to those who were in leadership in our particular fellowship of churches. Most of the time, superintendents or denominational church leaders visit local churches out of duty. The host pastors of the local congregations don't think much about a superintendent's monetary needs, because they typically receive a salary from the fellowship or denomination.

Yet, we began to show hospitality toward our fellowship's leaders and sow financial seed into their lives, giving them our very best offerings when they visited. When we did this, I began to see their gifts of ministry flow back incredibly into our church in a variety of ways.

PROMISE WITHOUT POTENTIAL

In Genesis 12:1-3, Abraham received a promise from God
that he was to become the father of many nations. God's
promise was incredible because Abraham lacked the
potential to be a father of one child—much less many
nations of children.

For years, Abraham roamed as a nomad with great wealth.
He had huge herds and flocks. He amassed great quantities
of silver and gold. He even had hundreds of laborers and
servants, yet he lacked an heir to the blessings that God had
provided for him.

His wife, Sarah had also reached a later season of her life.
Although still very beautiful and desirable enough for other
men to be extremely attracted to her (Genesis 12:10-20),
Sarah was too old to bear children.

In Genesis 18, we read where three divine visitors appeared
to Abraham near the great trees of Mamre. When Abraham
saw them, he hurried to meet them and humbled himself
before them. He asked permission to serve them by
washing their feet *(a wonderful ordinance of servanthood)*,
and he prepared a meal of the best food to refresh them. A
snack or a drive-through meal would not suffice. He sought
out his best calf and prepared a feast for his guests.

While the guests ate, one of the divine visitors inquired
about Abraham's wife. Then he gave Abraham this
promise:

> *"I will surely return to you about this time next
> year, and Sarah your wife will have a son."*
> *Genesis 18:10*

What happened?

All of Abraham's years of waiting, believing and even
working toward the promise had finally paid off. *(I don't*

mean this disrespectfully.) All Abraham's years of planting seed, expecting the harvest of a child, and his dream would soon be fulfilled. A son was to be born to Abraham and Sarah within the year.

The Bible goes on to say that Sarah laughed about the divine promise. She was overwhelmed with emotion. Then when the promise was fulfilled, Abraham and Sarah named their son *Isaac,* which means *laughter.* They were full of great joy.

After all of those years, Abraham's promise was released when he showed hospitality to those three visitors.

HOSPITALITY RELEASES POTENTIAL!

> *Do not forget to entertain strangers, for by so doing*
> *some people have entertained angels without*
> *knowing it.*   Hebrews 13:2

Here, the Bible says many have entertained angels without being aware of it. *To entertain* means *to receive as a guest; to show hospitality.*

God sends angels to men for a reason. Angels are commissioned to serve as messengers of God and to execute His purposes. When we show hospitality to angels, or to men who are messengers of God sent to execute His purposes, great potential is released.

We read the story in II Kings 4, where a well-to-do woman from Shunem practiced *The Law Of Hospitality* for Elisha every time he traveled through the region.

The woman spoke to her husband about Elisha's ministry. She expressed her confidence that he was a man of God. Upon receiving her husband's approval the woman had a room built onto their home, much like a garage apartment today. *(It's interesting to note that years ago, churches used to build rooms onto their buildings to lodge traveling evangelists. These add-ons were often called "prophet's chambers" because of this story in Scripture.)* Whenever Elisha would travel through, he would stay in the room which was built for him at the Shunammite's house.

One day, Elisha laid down in his bed and thought of all the kindness that he had received from the Shunammite woman. He called his servant Gehazi, and together they inquired about what they could do for her in return. (That's *The Law Of Mutual Benefit.)*

Elisha first asked if he could speak on her behalf to the king or the commander of the army. Elisha was very influential and favored among the government. But the Shunammite declined his offer, as she was already positioned with favor.

Then Gehazi informed Elisha that the woman did not have any children and that her husband was very old. After calling her to the doorway of the apartment, the prophet spoke this promise, "This time next year, you will have a son in your arms."

Practicing hospitality provides reproductive ability.

Both Abraham's wife Sarah, and the Shunammite woman had their dormant potential released through *The Law Of Hospitality.* They both received the promise of God and were able to reproduce with divine ability because of the honor showed to God's representatives.

I believe there is potential reserved in every person that can only be drawn upon through faith by acting on the principle of showing honor.

In contrast, the lack of hospitality can cost you greatly.

We cannot fully know the cost of our lack of hospitality in this life.

Pastor Tommy Barnett of Phoenix First Assembly (one of the largest churches in America) encourages ministers and laymen alike to enlarge what he calls their "circles of love." He says, "Those whom you exclude from your circle of love become your enemies." Through the principle of honor and hospitality, Pastor Barnett has enlarged his circle to include multiplied thousands of people.

> *When the Sabbath came, he began to teach in the synagogue, and many who heard him were amazed. "Where did this man get these things?" they asked. "What's this wisdom that has been given him, that he even does miracles! Isn't this the carpenter? Isn't this Mary's son and the brother of James, Joseph, Judas and Simon? Aren't his sisters here with us?" And they took offense at him. Jesus said to them, "Only in his hometown, among his relatives and in his own house is a prophet without honor." He could not do any miracles there, except lay his hands on a few sick people and heal them. And he was amazed at their lack of faith. Then Jesus went around teaching from village to village.*
>
> *Mark 6:2-6*

Isn't it amazing how we discredit those who live among us?

"They can't be special. They grew up with me," some say.

That was the attitude of people in the hometown of Jesus. They were offended at Him. They couldn't understand how His wisdom could be superior to their own. They wouldn't see the miracles as a testimony of his anointing. Their lack of honor cost them greatly.

Jesus couldn't do many miracles among those who did not practice hospitality.

Do you think Jesus was just having a bad day?

Maybe He didn't have his "A" game?

No, it was their offense that stopped the flow of the anointing.

He was amazed at their lack of faith.

Without faith, you can't receive anything from God. Salvation, healing, deliverance, provision and protection all come by faith.

> *Yet to all who received him, to those who believed in his name, he gave the right to become children of God.*   John 1:12

Let me explain this principle another way.

There is a line between respect and familiarity. When we cross that line, our relationships begin to deteriorate. This unseen line of respect—or honor—is drawn in every relationship we have, including our relationship with God.

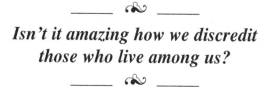

Isn't it amazing how we discredit those who live among us?

God commands that we honor His Name. The Jewish believers exercised this principle to the utmost. In fact, they would not even say God's name out loud. God never commanded them not to speak it; but He did command them to respect Him when they were speaking.

All throughout the Book of Leviticus, the Jews were taught to distinguish between what was holy and what was common. Even though the majority of us are not from Jewish descent, the principle of distinguishing the holy from the common is still something we should observe today.

In the New Testament, Paul writes that wives are to respect their husbands. He teaches that fathers should respect their children and not frustrate them.

I often see people who were raised in church, and their attendance, offerings and worship all become as common to them as going to a movie or a club. Unfortunately in much of the Church today, the dignity of worship and true respect for God has been lost.

Do not treat as common what God inhabits.

Our modern culture is much more casual than it was in times past. In many churches today pastors no longer wear coats and ties. While I understand the trend and am certainly not bound to tradition, I do not want to become casual in my attitude toward God's presence or His power. Nor do I want to treat God's people with familiarity. The "hometown syndrome" can creep into hearts and minds all too quickly and rob us of the anointing.

USE YOUR GIFTS TO SERVE OTHERS.

*Do you know that **you** are the temple of the Holy Spirit?*

God inhabits believers!

We should certainly show hospitality toward God, but we should also show hospitality toward other people, as well. We should honor them and use our gifts to serve them.

Whenever I travel to churches, I see that many Christians fail to show even common decency toward visitors. One of the services that I provide to other pastors is what I call "a walk through." I walk through their facilities with their staff members to help them develop creative thoughts on how to better serve their members and visitors.

I've also discovered that the Church is the only organization on earth that makes signs for those who already know where they're going! *(This is one of my pet peeves.)*

When a visitor first walks into a church, he usually stops in the foyer to look for directions. He invariably wants to remain anonymous, yet he usually can't, because he must ask for directions. There are no signs.

Even where there are signs in the church, they're usually written in code—for example: *Royal Rangers.*

What does that mean?

In some parts of the country, that could mean *the militia.*

Whenever I travel to a new city, I am forced to read road signs. The only way that I can get anywhere is to study the signs. *Signs should be for visitors!* The Bible says signs are for the unbelieving. *(Sorry—just a little church humor.)*

THE ANOINTING OF HOSPITALITY

In Scripture, the anointing oil was used for three purposes:

1. For sanctification—to set something, or someone, aside for divine use

2. For medicinal purposes—for healing of the sick

3. For hospitality—for refreshment, comfort and even aromatherapy

The prayers we raise up to God are described as the latter— a fragrant aroma to honor Him.

There is an anointing for hospitality. I have seen the gift of hospitality in the lives of many believers.

Paul referred to believers practicing *The Law Of Hospitality* in several places in his writings. He spoke of Gaius, his host while he traveled (Romans 16:23), and of some of the qualifications for widows to be cared for by the church, listing "showing hospitality," and "washing the feet of the saints," (I Timothy 5:10). Paul also commanded that believers should treat one another with honor and be given to hospitality (Romans 12:10, 13), and required that bishops practice this principle, as well (I Timothy 3:2, Titus 1:8).

When Jesus sent out the 72, he instructed them to qualify, or to disqualify, the towns by their hospitality. If the disciples were received, they were instructed to heal the sick and pronounce the coming of the kingdom of God.

If the townspeople did not welcome them, they were to shake the dust off their feet as a testimony against them. It is important to note that Jesus pronounced a greater judgment on these cities than the judgment Sodom received.

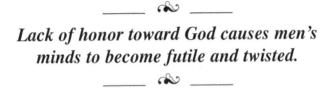

Lack of honor toward God causes men's minds to become futile and twisted.

Sodom was known for the perversion of homosexuality. If you examine the story of Sodom, you'll find that Lot found out about the impending judgment of God because he showed hospitality toward the messengers God sent to him.

The inhabitants of Sodom did not show hospitality. In fact, they were vile toward the divine visitors. Hospitality was held in such regard that Lot was willing to sacrifice the purity of his own daughters to keep the evil mob of men from their plot to molest God's messengers.

> *For although they knew God, they neither glorified him as God nor gave thanks to him, but their thinking became futile and their foolish hearts were darkened.*   *Romans 1:21*

The perversion of men's minds came about because, although they knew God, they didn't acknowledge Him or receive Him. Rejection of God—or lack of honor toward Him—causes men's minds to become futile and twisted.

CREATE AN ATMOSPHERE OF EXPECTATION.

I lived in a city where the leading industry is hospitality. This city hosts millions of visitors. Hospitality makes or breaks businesses every day there. Hotels compete with each other ruthlessly in the arena of customer service. The Hospitality Industry is huge there.

Of course, the standard-bearer in the city is Disney itself. Disney wrote the book on hospitality. Their theme song is: *"Be our guest. Be our guest. Put our service to the test."*

Disney knows that one person who is not shown hospitality can break down their entire system of return business. Hospitality is their bread and butter, so to speak.

The Disney philosophy includes seven elements that create an atmosphere of expectation.

1. Authority—Whenever a person arrives somewhere new, he must know that there is proper authority there. People interpret authority when they see order. Order means that there is a channel of authority.

2. Security—When a person sees order he feels secure. Security is becoming more and more important. In our "Post-9/11" world, we all look for secure areas.

3. Comfort—Creating an atmosphere of security establishes comfort. People are able to relax and feel at ease in a comfortable place.

4. Receptivity—People who are comfortable are able to receive.

5. Return—When a person receives something of value, they return.

6. Involvement—When a person returns, they become involved.

7. Reproduction—Involvement causes reproduction.

As a pastor, I've learned that when you start a church, you must accomplish these seven elements in order to have a second service. My team and I worked diligently to establish order, security and comfort before we ever opened the doors for our first service.

We had our nursery in order. Our workers were in uniform with identifying badges. We designed a registration process to ensure security.

From the outset, the parents felt comfortable leaving their precious children with us, because they saw order. The children felt comfortable, because they sensed security. (*Children pick up on insecurity immediately. Having novices serve in the nursery is one of the biggest mistakes that we make in the church.*)

When the first adults approached our doors, they were greeted and ushered to seats. They were welcomed without the threat of loosing their anonymity. The order in our services helped create an atmosphere that was both welcoming and exciting.

I also believe that the presence of the Holy Spirit is welcoming to people. In I Corinthians 14, Paul tells us that the Gifts of the Holy Spirit are for visitors. He also encourages us to have order in our services without the forbidding of speaking in tongues.

At the conclusion of our first service, we had seven adults and three children who made a spiritual decision to serve Christ. They received because they were comfortable.

It is unfortunate that many pastors have abandoned the manifestation of the Gifts of the Holy Spirit out of fear that visitors will be confused or offended. The Pentecostal church is the fastest-growing segment of Christianity in the world today, numbering more than 500 million people. Yet, in the United States, many pastors are avoiding the Pentecostal message for the sake of becoming *"Seeker Sensitive."* I can't disagree more with this philosophy.

The largest and fastest-growing churches in America are Pentecostal in their doctrine. Pentecost is the power behind a church driven by purpose.

Paul tells us, *"Follow the way of love and eagerly desire spiritual gifts...."* (I Corinthians 14:1).

Hospitality releases Spiritual Gifts.

God has given Spiritual Gifts to the Church. These gifts have the purpose of meeting needs that otherwise could not be met.

How are these gifts released?

The gifts flow when an atmosphere of hospitality is created.

POINTS FOR INCREASE:

Your potential is released through hospitality.

Use the gifts you have received to serve others.

Release the anointing of hospitality.

Create an atmosphere of expectation with hospitality.

4 The Law Of Reflex

*Teach them the decrees and laws, and show them
the way to live and the duties they are to perform.
But select capable men from all the people—men
who fear God, trustworthy men who hate dishonest
gain—and appoint them as officials over thousands,
hundreds, fifties and tens.   Exodus 18:20-21*

The Law Of Reflex creates systems to ensure an automatic
response to the environment of needs. There's no reason to
re-invent the wheel every time a need arises. Creative
thought should only be employed to ensure immediate
action when necessary.

Moses was given divine direction to fulfill his purpose. He
was born with a special destiny—to deliver God's people
out of the bondage of slavery. The circumstances
surrounding his birth, his upbringing in Pharaoh's palace,
his education and development of leadership skills by the
Egyptians were all designed by Divine Providence to bring
him to his destiny to lead God's people out of Egypt.

After the children of Israel were delivered once and for all
from Pharaoh, we find Moses leading the people and
serving them out of the gift that God had given him. It was
said of Moses that he knew God's ways (Psalm 103:7).

You are always in the superior position if you know the ways of God.

Moses knew God's ways because he asked God to reveal them to him. He spoke to the Lord and said, "You have told me to led these people but you have not told me how. Teach me your ways" (Exodus 33:12-13).

You must understand something about God. He is generous with wisdom. He freely gives wisdom to anyone who asks.

In the Book of James, we are told that we can "Count it all joy" when we are in a time of trial. The reason we are told this is because when we are in a trial, that's when we have the greatest opportunity to advance and to be completed through wisdom. When we seek God's way of doing things, we can live in victory through the turmoil and troubles of life.

> *When his father-in-law saw all that Moses was doing for the people, he said, "What is this you are doing for the people? Why do you alone sit as judge, while all these people stand around you from morning till evening?" Moses answered him, "Because the people come to me to seek God's will. Whenever they have a dispute, it is brought to me, and I decide between the parties and inform them of God's decrees and laws." Moses' father-in-law replied, "What you are doing is not good."*
> *Exodus 18:14-17*

Isn't it amazing to think that Moses, the man who received personal revelation from God, the man who was used as a prophet to write the Pentateuch, the man used to deliver God's people out from under Pharaoh's whip, was rebuked by his father-in-law, Jethro?

Jethro?

Who was he to speak to Moses that way?

The creators of the show, *The Beverly Hillbillies,* should be sued for misusing the name *Jethro.* In Hebrew, *Jethro* means *excellence* and *abundance.*

So, we could say that *"Excellence"* was speaking to Moses in verse 17, saying, *"What you are doing is not good."*

You won't hear everything you need to learn in prayer.

Some people think God speaks to us only through prayer. But that's just not true. God oftentimes will use other people to speak to us. He used Jethro to change Moses' entire way of thinking concerning leadership.

Wisdom is found in counsel.

Here are the seven principles Jethro gave Moses regarding *The Law Of Reflexive Ministry.* They can be regarded as "The Counsel Of *'Excellence:'"*

1. Represent the people to God. Moses knew God's ways. He knew how to communicate with God. No one could represent the people to God better than Moses.

2. Teach them the principles and laws. Instruct them in the truths of God's ways.

3. Show the people the way to live. Model leadership. Live it in front of them.

4. Release the duties that others should perform. Don't do it all yourself. You must release people into ministry.

5. Select capable men and qualify them. Don't just expect them to be trustworthy. Check them out. Test them if you must.

6. Appoint leaders at proven levels. Not everyone is qualified to lead at every level. If you put a man who is qualified for 100 over 50, he will grow that

level to 100. If you place a man who is capable of
50 over 100, he will shrink the 100 down to 50.

7. Let others make decisions. Share the load. Make
    only the difficult, untested decisions yourself.

What Jethro told Moses is one of the greatest leadership
lessons ever taught. We would do well to use these
principles as a model for any church, business or household.

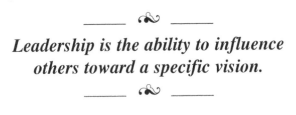

*Leadership is the ability to influence
others toward a specific vision.*

In the world today, we have a vacuum of leadership.
*Leadership is the ability to influence others toward a
specific vision.* That vision may be crafted by a church or
by a donut shop, but it takes leadership to bring people
together to make the vision come to pass.

CREATE SYSTEMS TO ENSURE AUTOMATIC RESPONSE TO NEEDS.

Let me explain how we employed this teaching at a large
church where I directed the pastoral ministries and was also
assigned the area of processing membership applications.

When I arrived to work at this church, one of my first
duties was to observe and review the new-membership
orientation. The orientation was held only occasionally and
was sporadic, at best.

When I showed up on a Sunday afternoon following our
three weekend services, I was amazed to see more than five
hundred applicants for membership. Half way through the
four hours of teaching, I sighed to myself, "What we are
doing is not good. We will only wear ourselves out and the

people will be worn out." The philosophy seemed to be, "Whosoever endures to the end will be a member."

The next day, I met with my staff to fix the problem. As we discussed the need for membership these things became obvious:

1. Membership should be available at any time.

2. Membership Application Packets should include a "Frequently Asked Question" sheet, and a video teaching of our doctrine, government and vision.

3. A staff member should be assigned to follow up on the process with each potential new member.

4. Membership Interviews with a pastor should be scheduled with potential members to allow us to "know those who labor among us."

5. Membership should be the gateway to involvement in ministry.

When we implemented this system, we were able to solve two critical issues. First, we were able to be more accessible to those wanting to join the church. Secondly, we were able to recruit workers for areas of ministry.

This reflexive system enabled us to qualify and recruit more than 100 new members a month, doubling the number of members previously welcomed into the church.

We also implemented *The Law Of Reflex* in our visitation program. Years ago, when I started my first church, I came up with the idea of delivering a bag of freshly baked cookies to our visitors. I saw this work wonderfully while establishing a new church.

When I went to serve at this mega-church, I wanted to implement this ministry there. My problem was obvious: How could I manage delivering a bag of cookies to the multitude of visitors each week?

I had to turn to *The Law Of Reflex*. We established "Zip Code Zones," and trained the visitation team to deliver the cookies. When the ushers received the visitor cards in the offering buckets, our team would sort the cards and gather the bags of cookies, which were made fresh in our school cafeteria, before the service was over. On departure from church, each visitation couple would grab the cookies for their zip code and make their deliveries.

I received notes of thanks regularly concerning the care and thoughtfulness visitors felt because of this simple act.

One couple who had visited our church was concerned that their children were not receiving instruction from the Bible during the services held at their small church. Although this bothered them, the parents didn't want to give up the friendliness of their small congregation.

Finally after hearing of all the wonderful programs our church offered for children, they decided to visit.

You can imagine their reservations. Our mega-church campus was the size of a shopping mall on hundreds of acres, but our parking attendants helped them navigate the parking lot. Greeters helped them feel at ease when they approached the building. Our registration system calmed their fears concerning leaving their children, and after the kids were placed in their classrooms, the couple found comfortable seats in the auditorium.

Of course they enjoyed the service. The excellence of the music ministry and the practical teaching from the pulpit helped them to feel good about their day.

As positive as their experience was, however, their fears of the size and scope of our church remained.

After enjoying lunch and sharing individual experiences of the church service, they returned home. When they walked toward the front door, a brightly colored gift bag awaited them with a card that read, *"Thank you for visiting our church today."*

They couldn't believe it. They had received a gift from us before they'd even returned home. This communicated something to them. The husband later said to me, "That church is this big for a reason. If you'd respond to my visit that fast, I believe you'd respond to my needs as fast, too." They joined our church shortly thereafter.

The larger you get, the faster you must become!

Just because you're large, you can't afford to be slothful. I've seen organizations grow too fast. You must not allow your growth to overtake your systems. You may be able to maintain your size for a while, but it will cost you in the long run, if you don't implement *The Law Of Reflex*.

I've seen churches and businesses grow beyond their abilities. Then when they try to catch up, the momentum begins to swing the other way. When that happens it's virtually impossible to turn around.

You will wear yourself out and the people will be worn out.

Think about all the processes that McDonald's has had to implement to keep up with their success. In order to maintain their growth, McDonald's has even had to demand that their farmers produce potatoes which match their exact specifications for french fries. (They can't afford to loose quality in their fries!)

McDonald's has learned that the larger that they get, the faster they have had to become.

If you're going to experience increase, *The Law Of Reflex* demands that you must get into the habit of birthing new ventures. However, when you birth a new project, you must allow it time to develop and mature before you go on to the next one. One pastor I know used to say, "You shouldn't have more than one baby in the crib at a time."

When it comes to giving birth to programs, you must birth, mature and release them into reflexive systems. The danger everyone faces at this stage is the temptation to expand too quickly. Doing so can distract you from your purposes.

GROWTH CAUSES PROBLEMS.

> *In those days when the number of disciples was increasing, the Grecian Jews among them complained against the Hebraic Jews because their widows were being overlooked in the daily distribution of food. So the Twelve gathered all the disciples together and said, "It would not be right for us to neglect the ministry of the word of God in order to wait on tables. Brothers, choose seven men from among you who are known to be full of the Spirit and wisdom. We will turn this responsibility over to them and will give our attention to prayer and the ministry of the word."*
>
> Acts 6:1-4

To experience growth, you will constantly be facing new and challenging problems. In this instance, the Grecians began to complain against the Hebrews regarding the widow ministry. This issue had a racial undertone.

An unanswered complaint to a legitimate problem can cause division.

THE PROCESS OF DIVISION

Have you ever noticed that churches often divide over seemingly small issues?

Usually, a church doesn't divide over doctrine, as most people would think. Most churches divide over smaller issues and unanswered problems. There are actually seven stages people go through which ultimately bring about division.

1. Murmuring

The first step toward division is the murmuring stage. This is when someone has a complaint and doesn't know how to deal with it properly. Although the complaint is legitimate, he resorts to the immature strategy of whining about it. The Grecians murmured against the Hebrews. The word for *murmuring* means *to mutter.* It also means *a secret displeasure not openly avowed.*

This reminds me of when I was a teenager, growing up in Oklahoma.

It was my responsibility to feed our cattle. I had to load the pick-up truck with hay bales and sacks of feed, and drive out into the fields in the winter. If I was late, the cows would begin to murmur. Of course the cattle couldn't voice their complaints to me personally, so they would begin to murmur to one another. *"Mooooooo-mooooooo,"* they'd mutter, until they received their feed.

Murmuring is never voiced to leadership directly. Often leaders don't hear the problem until it's too late. The Israelites fell into this trap many times. They were too insecure to approach God themselves, so they grumbled against the Lord.

This was frustrating to God. His conflicts with His people were often over their inability to properly address issues. They begged Moses to speak on their behalf and didn't want God to speak to them personally.

Many people have wondered why God stopped speaking directly to men with His voice. The answer is because men asked God to stop speaking to them.

2. Strife

If you don't address murmuring, complaints mature into strife. Strife is the *"rub"* you feel when you're near someone you have an issue with. It's the magnetic opposite. Instead of drawing toward one another, you repel each other.

In this stage, the complaint still goes unspoken. In fact, now the complainer *won't* speak to you—but make no mistake—he *will* speak to others. The Bible says that where there is strife, there is every evil work. A person at this level is in a dangerous position. He has allowed his complaint to become a bitter root. This causes him to take action.

3. Evil Work

The embittered person now takes action against leadership. His immaturity positions him to work against the leaders. He begins to strategize his offense. His scheming moves him into manipulation.

4. Manipulation

At this stage, the person begins to maneuver with his influence. He looks for a position or an office to force people to do things his way.

> *I know that after I leave, savage wolves will come in among you and will not spare the flock. Even from your own number men will arise and distort the truth in order to draw away disciples after them. So be on your guard! Remember that for three years I never stopped warning each of you night and day with tears.*   Acts 20:29-31

Paul says that these people *"draw"* others away. This is normal behavior for spiritual wolves. They draw people into isolation and away from truth, protection and the strength of fellowship.

5. Witchcraft

The process, which starts with murmuring, matures from "soulish" actions to a spiritual force of evil. The Bible says that bitterness in the heart causes a person to give place to the devil.

Most people don't know what witchcraft really is. The image of old hags brewing a concoction of poison in a pot is a false stereotype. *Witchcraft is the use of words—or even prayers—against leaders.* People in this stage are often deceived into thinking they're doing God's will.

People who practice witchcraft often feel spiritually superior. They feel guided by a divine call; however, they hate those in authority (Jude 8).

6. Rebellion

"Rebellion is as the sin of witchcraft," according to the Word (I Samuel 15:23 KJV). In this stage, a deceptive spirit, usurping the God-ordained authority of leaders begins to lead the individual. Sadly, the person in this phase has taken the way of Lucifer who sought to overthrow the throne of God.

Ezekiel tells us that the reason for Lucifer's fall was his arrogance. Pride filled his heart.

Can you imagine the absurdity of Lucifer?

He thought his beauty alone could give him the office of the Divine. Rebellion is a spirit that leads people to over-estimate their worth above established authority.

7. Division

The final step, which began with a simple muttering of a complaint, wickedly becomes division.

God hates this spirit.

It's the same spirit that causes divorce, separating the covenant bond of marriage. A marriage doesn't end suddenly. The beginning of the end is found in a murmur, which then becomes strife, evil work, manipulation, witchcraft and rebellion.

The divisive spirit is directly related to Lucifer's attempt to divide Heaven—he convinced one-third of the Heavenly host to follow him.

What was God's response?

God removed them from their positions of authority!

This process of division happens often in organizations and churches where associates are raised up with the founder or established leader. The associate begins to think of himself more highly than he should. He sets his sights on the high office. He covets power, prestige and privilege.

REFLEX PROTECTS THE PURPOSE.

How should you respond to complaints?

The disciples responded by keeping their focus on their purpose.

> *"It would not be right for us to neglect the ministry of the word of God [The Law Of Seed] in order to wait on tables."*   Acts 6:2b [Author's Note]

They realized that *The Law Of Seed* is the foundation of all increase. They knew they had to protect the Word as the first priority of their ministry.

Although everyone had sympathy for the widow ministry, the disciples did not elevate it above the purpose of the Word of God. The proposal to set up a reflexive system to meet the need pleased the whole group and the results were obvious.

> *So the word of God spread. The number of disciples in Jerusalem increased rapidly....*
> Acts 6:7a

The purpose of the Church is the ministry of God's Word. Remember: "Where the purpose is unknown, abuse is inevitable." *Where the purpose is not protected, abuse is guaranteed.*

Don't confuse activity with productivity.

I learned as a young pastor that ministry programs are a dime a dozen. You always have more vision than provision. People constantly approached me to birth new ministries. I found many of them took away from the main purpose of our church—the Sunday morning service.

I have challenged pastors, businessmen and homemakers alike, to keep things *off* their calendars. *Don't confuse activity with productivity.* There's a big difference.

> *And the things you have heard me say in the presence of many witnesses entrust to reliable men who will also be qualified to teach others.*
> *II Timothy 2:2*

Paul received revelation from the Lord, then he taught Timothy. Timothy taught qualified men who would teach others. This process ensured four generations of teachers!

Pastor Yonggi Cho implemented a reflexive system of teaching. He built the world's largest church by establishing his ministry on Exodus 18.

Pastor Cho suffered a major illness due to exhaustion from growing a church beyond its systems of management. It took years to overcome his illness. On his sick bed, he conceived the reflexive system of cell-group ministry, which has revolutionized church growth around the world.

Thousands of churches have duplicated this system of discipleship. The results are amazing. Millions have come into the kingdom.

Everything runs full circle doesn't it?

What has been will be again.

The Church started out in houses. Now after 2,000 years of Church history, the Church has returned to homes.

The key to growth is employing reflexive systems. The same is true in your business or in your personal life.

What are you presently doing that you could pass on to those around you?

Do what only you can do, and release others to do what they can do through *The Law Of Reflex.*

POINTS FOR INCREASE:

Create systems of automatic response to needs.

*Realize that growth causes problems,
but reflex solves them.*

Division is a process.

Protect your purpose.

5 The Law Of Mutual Benefit

But seek first his kingdom and his righteousness,
and all these things will be given to you as well.
                                                    Matthew 6:33

The Law Of Mutual Benefit guarantees that each party in a relationship experiences increase. Many corporations lose sight of this law and forfeit their success. Wal-Mart sells for less. That's their statement of mutual benefit, and by it, they have become the largest company in the world.

Most people never approach their relationship with God with this law in mind. Yet, the Gospel operates by *The Law Of Mutual Benefit.*

The question, "What's in it for me?" doesn't intimidate God.

I know that this is shocking and may be taken the wrong way, but stop and think about it: God wants you to be bold enough to ask. *"You do not have, because you do not ask"* (James 4:2).

David, a lowly shepherd boy, certainly wasn't intimidated to ask King Saul, "What will be done for the man who slays this giant?"

The promise of great wealth, freedom from taxation and the king's daughter spurred David on through a great challenge.

CRISIS BRINGS OPPORTUNITY.

When you are facing a crisis or challenge, follow David's example:

1. Use what you have proven. Don't try to use someone else's strategies or experiences, or try to assume another's faith.

2   Recall past victories. You have overcome challenges before. How did you do it? How did God help you? It may have been a smaller battle, but it was a lesson for you.

3. Remember your position in Christ. You have a covenant with God through Jesus Christ! You are an overcomer, a victor and more than a conqueror.

4. Don't be afraid to ask, "What will be done for the man...?" Any business deal works this way.

    In any endeavor, the question is not *"Can* I do it?" but *"Will* I do it?" C*an* is an article of ability. W*ill* is an article of desire, emotion and commitment. David told the king, "Not only *can* I take out the giant, but I *will* defeat him."

    The benefit for Israel was the defeat of their mortal enemy. The mutual benefit for David was the reward, the positioning and the fulfillment of his destiny.

GOD BELIEVES IN THE REWARD SYSTEM.

Anyone who receives instruction in the word must share all good things with his instructor.
                              Galatians 6:6

If we are going to make increase happen, we must also share in that increase.

I have practiced partnership with ministers who have taught me down through the years. It is thrilling to hear teaching from God's Word, so I look for opportunities to sow financially back into ministries whenever I can.

This is important! I have learned that when I sow financially into a teaching ministry I have received from, a new level of relationship is opened to me. Financial seed releases new insight.

> ...*The one who sows to please the Spirit, from the Spirit will reap eternal life.*   Galatians 6:8b

My wife and I have seen *The Law Of Mutual Benefit* work in our lives in planting churches. We have walked in obedience to what God has called us to do, even when we did not have the finances to do so.

When God called us to start a church in Mobile, Alabama, we didn't have any money, yet I knew that I had heard from God. I was intimidated by the task. But within one year of starting our church, God supernaturally allowed us to build our dream home.

> *"I tell you the truth," Jesus replied, "no one who has left home or brothers or sisters or mother or father or children or fields for me and the gospel will fail to receive a hundred times as much in this present age (homes, brothers, sisters, mothers, children and fields—and with them, persecutions) and in the age to come, eternal life.*
> *Mark 10:29-30*

That's *The Law Of Mutual Benefit*. Jesus says that if we leave someone or something for His sake, He will repay us with interest. If you lay down a home for the sake of the

Gospel, you'll receive a better home. If you leave a field of sown seed, you will receive a better harvest!

I have had to bank on this promise, because, in the past, God has called me to leave what He first called me to plant. These were hard decisions, yet because of this promise, I could be willingly obedient, and even joyful at the prospect.

Because of this promise, my wife has willingly laid down her dream home three times, in order to be obedient to God's call and direction in our lives.

God calls us to greater opportunities.

Some have shipwrecked their faith because they became embittered at God's calling. Some have resented His timing in their lives. I have known people who are confused and believe that God's call is a burden.

When God is calling you to do something, He is calling you to greater opportunities. *He calls you to step up—not down—to enlarge, to increase and to expand your life.*

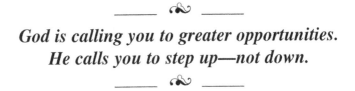

God is calling you to greater opportunities.
He calls you to step up—not down.

The rich, young ruler Jesus tried to recruit failed to understand this principle. The man had religious conviction. (He had kept the Law from his childhood). He was successful and had become wealthy (by being obedient to the precepts and principles of God). He worked the Word and the Word worked for him. However, when Jesus instructed him to sell his possessions and give everything to the poor, the young man stumbled. It was too much to ask. He allowed comfort to keep him from increase.

Jesus knew His present treasurer (Judas) would betray Him. He needed a man to be in a position to take over that part of His ministry.

Who would have qualified better than this rich, young ruler?

Mark 10:29-30 would have guaranteed him a hundredfold return on his investment.

Jesus believes in the reward system.

> *The man who plants and the man who waters have one purpose, and each will be rewarded according to his own labor.*   I Corinthians 3:8

Each person has a contribution to make to the system of the Gospel. The laborer is worthy of his hire. God commands us to be fair and honest with our employees. If He demands that of us, then surely He will keep His own laws. God will reward us for our work.

When Jesus taught the parable of the talents, the master returned and rewarded the faithful servants with joy and a share of the master's happiness.

Jesus said that upon His return, He would bring our reward with Him (Matthew 16:27). He is recording the minutest detail of our giving (Mark 9:41).

Some have "thrown out the baby with the bath water," when it comes to understanding Biblical prosperity. For every mile of road, there are two miles of ditch. You can be in the ditch on either side of the road, but you're still in the ditch.

The same is true in the excess of teaching. You can have error through *emphasis*. Some have aborted the genuine teaching of Biblical prosperity because others have abused it for personal gain.

Pastor Yonggi Cho faced a great challenge in building a church facility for his growing congregation after the devastation of the Korean War. In order to build a building, Pastor Cho realized that he had to first build his people. He began to teach them Biblical prosperity in order to liberate them from poverty. Even when fellow ministers pressured him to stop teaching prosperity, he pressed on. Now hundreds of thousands of Korean believers have been released from the terrible bondage of poverty. Thousands have become self-made millionaires within his congregation.

The greatest challenge to people's thinking is their narrow understanding of Biblical prosperity.

In Hebrew, the word *prosperity* means *to rush* or *to advance, to make progress, to succeed, to make profitable.* The Greek word for *prosper* means *to be led in a direct and easy way.*

Prosperity does not mean money!

Money is simply a byproduct of a prosperous life. Getting money is not the motive of the prosperous person; it isn't the objective. Money is a currency of exchange—nothing more—nothing less. It is the ability to make your way. *Your way* is what is important in life.

Are you able to live your purpose and destiny?

Are you free to do what God has called you to do?

Some of the most frustrated people I know are those who have *means without meaning.*

You often see this lived out by children of the privileged. Drugs, alcohol and sexual promiscuity destroy their lives because they do not have the appetite for purpose. Remember: "Where the purpose is unknown, abuse is inevitable."

Bill Gates, the wealthiest man on earth, has announced his intentions to leave only a fraction of his accumulated wealth to his children, choosing to give his billions away through an established charity. Some question his reasoning, but I understand it. By doing so, he is actually protecting his children's lives.

> *An inheritance quickly gained at the beginning will not be blessed at the end.*   Proverbs 20:21

Proverbs 16:26 says the laborer's appetite works for him because his hunger drives him on. People who lack an appetite lack self-preservation.

Equal to the frustration of those who have *means without meaning,* are those who have *meaning without means.*

The missionary who has an assignment to reach nations is most frustrated when he is forced to spend months raising funds for ministry. The pastor who has the vision for a larger facility to accommodate winning souls, spends nights awakened with anxiety.

I'm going to say something that may sound contradictory at first, but—**it is the wisdom of God that we don't always have the money when we think we need it.**

Facing lack causes us to seek God for direction. When we seek His wisdom, creativity is released through us. The windows of Heaven are open, and Heaven's currency is poured out upon us.

God doesn't counterfeit money. He doesn't operate in our economy. God's currencies are wisdom, knowledge, witty inventions, favor, blessings and ideas. We must exchange the currency of Heaven for the currency of man.

The conception of creativity is crisis!

Years ago, my ministry built several churches in Honduras. When we arrived in San Pedro Sula, we went to a bank to exchange American dollars for Honduran currency. We did this in order to have the best rate of exchange. If we had kept our American money and used it to purchase items on the street, we wouldn't have received a very favorable exchange.

This principle works with Heaven's currency. When you receive an idea, you must convert it! When you receive knowledge, you must use it! When you receive a witty invention, you must patent it!

Have you ever had an idea and let it go without doing anything, and then a few months later seen your idea packaged and being sold in stores?

I've read books others have written that I was supposed to write. I sat, waited and procrastinated with the thoughts while others picked up a pen and wrote them down.

A few months after I started my first church, I had seven ministers tell me that they had each felt called to start a church in the same city but didn't do it. These men were better positioned and had more experience than I did. But I had something that they didn't—I was hungry. My appetite drove me to work.

THE TEMPTATION OF COMFORT

Terah was the father of three sons, Abram, Nahor and Haran. Terah had it in his heart to go to Canaan. While he journeyed toward his destination, Terah stopped in Haran. Haran was a city named after his third son who had died a tragic death. The Bible says that Terah settled there. Instead of pressing on to his destiny, Terah didn't want to leave the memorial place of his son. The name *Terah* means *delay,* or *station.*

Many people face challenges, devastations, losses or deaths that they simply won't leave behind. These places of memorial provide a comfortable place of refuge. These comfort stations may hinder us, or cause us to delay our destiny.

God challenged Abram to leave his father to go to Canaan. Sometimes, we have to forsake our family members to move on toward destiny (Mark 10:29). The prosperous person knows this.

> *By faith Abraham, when called to go to a place he would later receive as his inheritance, obeyed and went, even though he did not know where he was going.*   *Hebrews 11:8*

It requires faith to answer God's call and leave our comfort stations in life.

Have you been called out of your comfort zone?

Have you chosen to settle?

The person who understands God's *Law Of Mutual Benefit* possesses something greater than money. He has the confidence of provision. He has the ability to trust that his needs will be met daily, as he journeys toward his destiny. The prayer of Jesus, "Give us today our daily bread," becomes the constant confession of the prosperous soul.

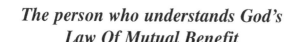

The person who understands God's Law Of Mutual Benefit possesses something greater than money.

The Law Of Mutual Benefit teaches that, as we pursue God's divine destiny for our lives, our desires and deepest dreams will be fulfilled.

Because Abraham was willing and obedient to leave his father and to pursue the promise, his descendants populate the earth. His children cross every racial barrier. Those who live by faith are born into his family (Romans 4:16).

As you step out of your comfort zone, you'll need to rely on faith like never before. You'll need a daily dose of God's reassurance. It will require that every step you take, be taken with wisdom and insight. God told Abraham that every step he took claimed possession of the promise (Genesis 13:17).

As you go, remember that nowhere in Scripture are you told to take a leap of faith.

STEPS VS. LEAPS

> *The steps of a good man are ordered by the LORD: and he delighteth in his way.*
> *Psalms 37:23 KJV*

God guides our *steps,* not our leaps. It was the devil who tempted Jesus to take a leap off the pinnacle of the Temple to test the Father's love.

God directs you through daily leadership. He leads you in *the direction* of your destiny, but the direction is not the same as the destiny. As God leads you, you may go toward something only to find out that once you got there, it was not the objective. It was only a visual landmark to get you into place for the next direction.

Let me give you an example. My wife and I used to hide Easter eggs for our kids to find on the holiday. When our children were very little, I would help them find the eggs. I wouldn't find the eggs for them, but I would give them direction. I might tell my youngest child, Courtney, "Go over by that tree." I knew that once she got close to the tree, she'd be able to see the egg. It wouldn't make sense for me to say, "Go toward the egg." She couldn't see the egg, but she could see the tree.

God may tell you to go toward something you presently see, so that you will be able to see something that is presently hidden from you.

I pursue the will of God knowing that *The Law Of Mutual Benefit* works for me. I realize that as I move toward what I know, I will learn more of God's plan. I now know in part; then I will know fully.

It's God's delight to reveal His secrets to you.

GOD'S NOT HIDING SOMETHING *FROM* YOU. HE'S HIDING SOMETHING *FOR* YOU.

> *He replied, "The knowledge of the secrets of the kingdom of heaven has been given to you...."*
> *Matthew 13:11a*

We have the benefit of knowing and receiving insight into God's plan, as we work His plan on the earth.

> *Surely the Sovereign LORD does nothing without revealing his plan to his servants the prophets.*
> *Amos 3:7*

Why does God reveal His plan to prophets first?

So that they will do what prophets do—so they'll proclaim the will of God on the earth. Prophets prophesy!

The Law Of Mutual Benefit worked for the prophet, Elijah. He was faithful to prophesy a famine because of King Ahab's wickedness.

> *Now Elijah the Tishbite, from Tishbe in Gilead, said to Ahab, "As the LORD, the God of Israel, lives, whom I serve, there will be neither dew nor rain in the next few years except at my word." Then the word of the LORD came to Elijah: "Leave here, turn eastward and hide in the Kerith Ravine, east of the Jordan. You will drink from the brook, and I*

*have ordered the ravens to feed you there." So he
did what the LORD had told him. He went to the
Kerith Ravine, east of the Jordan, and stayed there.
The ravens brought him bread and meat in the
morning and bread and meat in the evening, and he
drank from the brook. Some time later the brook
dried up because there had been no rain in the
land.   I Kings 17:1-7*

The prophecy had a direct effect on Elijah. He would have
faced starvation, if it were not for God's daily provision.
God provided a brook for Elijah to drink from. He also
directed ravens to deliver meat to the prophet twice each
day.

But then the brook dried up.

**When a stream of income in your life dries up, don't
morn the former supply of God, but look for direction to
find a new source of supply.**

*Then the word of the LORD came to him: "Go at
once to Zarephath of Sidon and stay there. I have
commanded a widow in that place to supply you
with food."   I Kings 17:8-9*

God gave Elijah new direction for supply. A widow was in
need in the town of Zarephath. She and her son were
facing death, so God moved Elijah to intervene on their
behalf.

God said, "I've commanded a widow to feed you."

Sounds great doesn't it?

However, the widow *didn't know* that she was commanded.

When the prophet asked the widow what she was preparing
to do, she said, "I'm about to prepare a last meal for my son
and I to eat, so that we may die."

*Elijah said to her, "Don't be afraid. Go home and
do as you have said. But first make a small cake of
bread for me from what you have and bring it to
me, and then make something for yourself and your
son."*   *I Kings 17:13*

The prophet said, "First prepare a cake for me."

Then he did what prophets do—he prophesied provision for
the widow.

*"For this is what the LORD, the God of Israel,
says: 'The jar of flour will not be used up and the
jug of oil will not run dry until the day the LORD
gives rain on the land.'" She went away and did as
Elijah had told her. So there was food every day
for Elijah and for the woman and her family. For
the jar of flour was not used up and the jug of oil
did not run dry, in keeping with the word of the
LORD spoken by Elijah.*   *I Kings 17:14-16*

God has provision for you, but you must follow the streams
of income that He moves you to.

The prophet Elijah's provision was found when he fulfilled
his assignment of prophesying. He lived by the fruit of his
lips.

As a minister of the Gospel, my supply is in direct
proportion to the teaching and preaching of God's Word.
As I share the seed of the Word of God, I become a partaker
in the harvest it produces. Just as baking more bread
increases a baker's income, and treating more patients
increases a doctor's income, enlarging his audience
increases a minister's income.

Why does God want to reveal His plan to you?

So that you will do what you're to do on the earth.

What good is it for you to get to know God's will only after you die?

God wants you to know His good, and pleasing, and perfect will now, so that you can do it (Romans 12:2).

POINTS FOR INCREASE:

The Law Of Mutual Benefit guarantees that each party in a relationship experiences increase.

A crisis can be an opportunity that will position you for purpose.

God believes in the reward system.

The greatest temptation against the accomplishment of your dream is comfort.

Nowhere in Scripture are we told to take a leap of faith.

God is not hiding something from you. He's hiding something for you.

6 The Law Of Faith To Follow

"Come, follow me," Jesus said, "and I will make you fishers of men."   *Matthew 4:19*

It requires faith to follow a vision. *The Law Of Faith To Follow* gives us the ability to see the vision God has for us become a reality. Jesus knew how to give His disciples faith to follow.

"Leadership is influence."—John Maxwell

Most people struggle with getting people to follow them.

Did you ever wonder why?

It's because leadership means that you must exercise influence. If you're going to lead people, you must be confident that you have something to offer them and somewhere to take them. Jesus offered His disciples both.

Jesus said, *"Follow me and I will make you..."*

RECRUITMENT VS. VOLUNTEERISM

Notice how the disciples became followers of Jesus. He recruited them. Jesus never asked for volunteers!

When Jesus recruited people, He didn't go to the religious people of that day. He went to the employed.

He recruited fishermen, a doctor and even a tax collector. Jesus walked straight up to them and called them out of their secular employment. He offered *to make them* into what they were born to become. Jesus knew how to recruit workers.

If you are a leader, you should go after the employed. That's right. Go after those who are already busy. I've learned that if I ask for volunteers, I usually only get the religious minded.

The religious minded are those who are motivated by guilt or by a "salvation-by-works" mentality. Their motivation often is short lived. They become frustrated when they don't receive what they feel is their due recognition. They bail out when the going gets tough.

By actively recruiting followers, you are able to attract the capable—not just the available. *Many people are available for a reason.* When you recruit, you get the gifted—not just the religious or flaky.

Some churches are so desperate for workers, they're willing to compromise their standards in order to fill the often-unglamorous positions. Some pastors have even inadvertently allowed pedophiles to get into their ranks, because they were so hard up for children's workers, they didn't qualify them first.

Never allow anyone to work with juveniles without conducting a thorough background check on them first. We have stopped hundreds of child molesters from getting a position among us with this simple procedure.

I believe that church membership should be the qualifying process toward ministry. Membership should have responsibilities, not just privileges. In most churches, however, membership is based upon the democratic rule of government—not the qualifying of people for ministry. In

our membership system, we have a built-in recruitment
system to fill positions of ministry in the church.

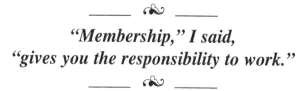

"Membership," I said, "gives you the responsibility to work."

I remember one day in my church, as I concluded a
membership interview with a couple, I asked, "What area of
ministry would you like to be considered and trained for?"

The gentlemen responded, "Well, I just want to be a
member so that I can vote."

I informed him that he apparently misunderstood the
purpose of church membership. "Membership," I said,
"gives you the responsibility to work, not just the privilege
to vote."

**The unhappiest people in any community are the
unemployed.**

If you are building a church or a business, you must believe
in what you are doing enough to recruit the gifted. You
should go after the best, the brightest and the brilliant.

FAITH VS. NEED

I hope that I don't shock your religious thinking by this
statement, however, it's important to understand what
motivates God to action.

Need alone does not move God!

Okay. Catch your breath.

Now, think about it. If needs moved God, then He would
fill them immediately. We wouldn't have any needs, if God
was moved to action solely because we had problems.

Are you still with me?

So what moves God to act on your behalf?

The answer is found in Hebrews 11:6.

> *And without faith it is impossible to please God,*
> *because anyone who comes to him must believe that*
> *he exists and that he rewards those who earnestly*
> *seek him.*   *Hebrews 11:6*

Faith moves God's hand.

Let me give you an example of how to get God's attention.

> *When Jesus had again crossed over by boat to the*
> *other side of the lake, a large crowd gathered*
> *around him while he was by the lake. Then one of*
> *the synagogue rulers, named Jairus, came there.*
> *Seeing Jesus, he fell at his feet and pleaded*
> *earnestly with him, "My little daughter is dying.*
> *Please come and put your hands on her so that she*
> *will be healed and live." So Jesus went with him.*
> *A large crowd followed and pressed around him.*
>   *Mark 5:21-24*

Jesus had just arrived, when a large crowd of people gathered around Him.

Do you suppose that within that large crowd there were any people with needs present?

Do you think that someone within that crowd had something that Jesus could do for them?

Certainly those people had needs. *And not only did they have needs—Jesus knew what their needs were.*

Jairus had a need. But Jairus did something different. In desperation, he approached Jesus, worshipped him and petitioned him with sincerity. "My daughter is dying. Please come and heal her."

And Jesus went with him.

Faith moves God to action.

As Jesus was going to answer Jairus' request, the large mob of people pressed against Him. Within that crowd of people, a woman, who had been bleeding for twelve years, reached out to touch Jesus as He passed by her.

Notice, that she didn't want the attention of Jesus! She wanted to go unnoticed. She wanted healing without exposure. She reasoned in her heart that if she could simply touch Him as He passed by, she would be healed.

When her faith moved her to action, she touched Jesus and withdrew virtue, or power, from Him. The faith of Jesus wasn't even used in her situation. *Her faith* healed her.

Faith moves God's hand.

What I want you to see in these two cases is that both Jairus and the woman had needs that were met *by faith.* Jesus did not answer their requests simply because they had needs.

Likewise, people are not motivated by needs. People are motivated by faith.

Seeing needs may move people to action initially, but soon compassion wanes for the overwhelming need. Jesus said, "The poor you will always have among you, but you will not always have me." If people were moved solely on the basis of need, there wouldn't be any poor in the world today.

When I was a young teenager, I watched a program about starving children. I was so moved by compassion that I dialed the phone number on the screen and pledged to help.

I had good intentions. I was moved to action. However, soon the pictures of those children began to fade and were crowded out by the daily issues of my life. I forgot about them.

A few years later, I was in college. I heard about a program which helped poverty-stricken children in Latin America. This time, I was moved with compassion by the needs, but something greater gripped me. The leaders of the program showed me results. They showed me what happened to a child after he received a $24-a-month pledge. They gave me faith to follow. They cast a vision and equipped me with hope.

When you recruit gifted people, you must give them hope. Hope is a vision. It's a picture of what can be accomplished.

Do you remember when a group of secular recording artists united to help the cause of starving people under the banner, *We Are The World?*

They sacrificially joined their efforts to produce a record album, sang anthems of the hurting, and exposed the needs of hungry people. Yet, they're not still singing today about those countries.

What happened to their cause?

The need proved greater than their faith.

JESUS DOES NOT EXPECT US TO WORK ON EMPTY. HE EQUIPS THOSE HE RECRUITS.

After His death, Jesus appeared to His disciples and told them that, before they were to fulfill their assignments, they were to receive empowerment for the task. He said, "Wait until you receive power" (Acts 1:8).

Jesus does not expect us to attempt anything without being empowered to accomplish it.

If you want people to follow you, you must give them a vision. You must give them faith. You can't just show them the need. You have to empower them to fill it. When you have a large task or a great exploit to be done, you must prepare your people to accomplish it.

I may receive a vision from God, but I must turn and give that vision to those who follow me. I must give them faith to follow.

How do I give them faith?

> *So then faith cometh by hearing, and hearing by the word of God.*   Romans 10:17 KJV

I give them the Word.

Many pastors struggle with casting vision for new projects, programs or buildings because they cast the need, instead of giving people faith. They reason, "Can't people see that we need this?"

Yes, people see the need, but your need alone cannot move people through the struggles and challenges sacrificial giving requires. As soon as the pressure comes *(and it always comes)*, people give up because they are **not** empowered by need. People are only empowered by faith!

Faith moves people. Faith moves mountains. Faith brings rewards.

Need-based recruitment doesn't move people to action. You can see this failure displayed whenever a pastor tries to get volunteers for children's ministry or the nursery in his church. Think about what we are asking people to do. We're asking them to give up enjoying a worship service so that they can baby sit and change diapers in a small, smelly room.

Who would want to do that?

There is usually one lady who gets stuck with the task of caring for the children—and I mean stuck. She's been back there for forty years. She's usually old and mean and she feels totally unnoticed and unappreciated.

The pastor is finally forced to try to help her or to replace her (only when she is physically unable to carry the burden). He approaches the pulpit with the daunting task of asking the mothers of the church—or even forcing them by guilt—to volunteer.

"Ladies, we've got to get some help with these kids in the nursery. Sister Mary just can't handle it any more."

Usually, this approach fails to get new workers. The pastor reacts with discouragement and defeat, thinking that his people are just not committed.

The pastor's problem is that the people see the nursery as a need. They don't have any faith that their commitment will result in anything. They don't see their time as an investment in a ministry with eternal rewards.

On the other hand, the wise pastor will present his congregation with a vision for reaching children.

"There will never be a minister who can take the place of the first person who introduces a child to the Lord. Jesus promised eternal rewards for those who bless children in His Name. Who would like to go down in Heaven's records as being the first person who ever introduced these children to Jesus?"

The question is, *who wouldn't?*

Faith motivates people!

COMMUNICATE THE VISION IN SIMPLE TERMS.

The vision must be made clear for people to run with it.

Vision is powerful. Vision is the ability to see an image of the unreal. **Vision is when your inward senses get a glimpse of your possible future.**

One day as I was preparing a teaching series about vision, I immediately reached for one of my many books on the subject. I took the book down off the shelf, however, I felt the Lord urging me to put it back and to begin to pray. As I obeyed, I felt impressed to look at the story of Noah. What I found there was life changing.

Noah was given the difficult task of building an ark to save his family and a cargo of animals from the greatest disaster known to mankind—the global flood that killed every living creature on earth. Noah's motivation wasn't just to fulfill God's command, but to rescue his family, as well.

Following the flood, God commanded Noah and his family to be fruitful and increase in number to fill the earth.

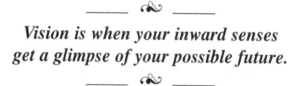

Vision is when your inward senses get a glimpse of your possible future.

God's plan was to use the seed of Noah to repopulate the earth. (There's *The Law Of Seed* at work again.)

Years later, the descendants of Noah's three sons settled in Shinar—the plains of modern-day Iraq—and they began to build a city. They used creativity and engineering to establish themselves.

> *Then they said, "Come, let us build ourselves a city, with a tower that reaches to the heavens, so that we may make a name for ourselves and not be scattered over the face of the whole earth."*
> *Genesis 11:4*

This statement defines their mission.

Any corporation would be proud to have such a clearly defined reason for being. It states their objective, their strategy and their purpose.

Furthermore, God, Himself, marveled when He saw the building. He said, "If they have begun to do this in unity, speaking the same language, then nothing they plan to do will be impossible for them" (Genesis 11:6).

What an amazing compliment. God said that they could have accomplished the impossible!

Now I know that the story of the Tower of Babel is a commentary on the wicked aspirations of fallen man, but there is also a principle here that we can turn to be positive in accomplishing works for the Lord.

I asked the Lord about His statement and He said, "Look at the three sons of Noah and you will see the three steps that accomplish vision."

The three sons of Noah were Shem, Ham and Japheth. Their descendants are listed in Genesis 10, in what is referred to as the Table of Nations. Out of Noah's three sons the whole earth was repopulated.

In Hebrew, *Shem* means *name,* which suggests *reputation, report,* and *influence. Ham* literally means *hot,* which carries the connotation *to sweat, to labor,* and *to toil.* Japheth means *open,* indicating *to extend, to enlarge, to stretch* or *to reach.*

The three steps to accomplish any vision are revealed in the mission statement of Tower of Babel project:

"Come let us **build** *(Ham)* a city with a tower that **reaches** *(Japheth)* to the heavens, so that we may make a **name** *(Shem)* for ourselves."

Let me explain it this way: If you're going to accomplish a vision you will need three types of people—the *Hams*, the *Shems* and the *Japheths*.

1. The *Hams* are people who became skilled laborers, craftsmen. The Bible records that Ham's descendants (the Canaanites) actually became the slaves, or hard laborers, for the descendants of Ham's brothers, Shem and Japheth.

2. In order to accomplish any vision, you also need the *Shems*. Shem was very powerful. The *Shems* of today are influential and powerful, and they usually have financial abilities.

3. *Japheths* are people who always want to reach out to extend beyond the boundaries. They are open-minded. They want to get "out of the box."

The key to accomplishing the impossible is to have all three types of people represented in the project. You need people who desire to reach beyond the status quo. You must have financiers. You must also have skilled laborers to do the work.

Some have speculated as to why God was upset with their vision to build a tower to reach into the heavens. I believe the answer is obvious.

Men make plans, but God's purposes prevail.

The people at Babel had a vision for themselves that was contrary to God's purposes for them. He said, "Populate the earth, fill it, and increase." They said, "Let's not be scattered."

The underlying truth behind the story is that these three people groups could only accomplish the impossible when they understood each other. Once communication is interrupted, men "Babel." To stop their plan, God simply confused their communication.

(For more information on the three sons of Noah go to www.NeilKennedyMinistries.com.)

Vision must be communicated. It must be understood.

Educators take a simple truth and make it hard. *Communicators* take a hard truth and make it simple.

> *"Write down the revelation and make it plain on tablets so that a herald may run with it."*
> *Habakkuk 2:2b*

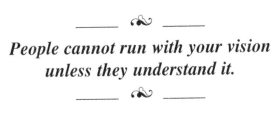

People cannot run with your vision unless they understand it.

The Law Of Faith To Follow requires that we make the vision simple. Simplicity doesn't indicate a lack of intellect. On the contrary, simplicity indicates wisdom.

Jesus communicated through the use of parables to explain the complicated truths of God's kingdom. How many sermons have been preached—how many books have been written espousing the wisdom of His parables? Parables of farming, lost coins or fishing, are simple illustrations people can relate to, yet they teach amazing spiritual principles.

People cannot run with your vision unless they understand it. They will stumble unless they can communicate it themselves.

President John F. Kennedy articulated in the simplest terms his vision to accomplish the most difficult task known to man in his time. He said, "I believe that this nation should commit itself to achieving the goal, before this decade is out, of landing a man on the Moon and returning him safely to earth."

That was an amazing statement of vision! His statement worked because it was simple, precise and powerfully energizing.

President Kennedy did not tell the nation of the enormous financial challenge, the ingenious engineering, or the potential devastation that could occur. He simply said, in one sentence, the vision that motivated an entire country's resources.

Jesus said, "Go into all the world and preach the good news to all creation." With this statement the Church received her mission, her message, and the meaning of her existence.

AUTHORITY FLOWS THROUGH LEADERSHIP.

Never assume that someone knows what you know.

I have learned that God doesn't speak to those under me in the same way that He speaks to me. I used to assume that my staff heard from God the same way I heard from Him, but after years of leading people, I now realize that God will not go around my leadership to speak to people under me. God honors lines of authority.

When I founded Eastern Shore Christian Center, I started alone. I did not have a ministry team. As the ministry grew, I hired different ministers and staff to work with me. Many times I failed to understand that God did not communicate my vision with them. They didn't know it. My frustrations with them were often based on my assumption that they knew what I knew.

You can imagine my insecurity when different people, from time to time, would approach me saying, "God told me this or that."

I would wonder, "Why didn't God speak to me about that?"
I was confused. I prayed, "Lord, why didn't I hear from
You about this?"

God will not speak around you. He does not gossip or
slander you. If He's put you in leadership, He is well able
to lead you.

> *My sheep listen to my voice; I know them, and they*
> *follow me.*   John 10:27

Until I learned this lesson, I could be easily confused by
what I call *WTS—Wagging Tongue Syndrome.*

WTS is a plague in the modern-day Pentecostal/Charismatic
church. God said through Jeremiah the prophet, "I'm
against the prophets who wag their tongues and say, 'The
Lord declares...'" (Jeremiah 23:31).

People don't consider how evil it is to quote God when He
didn't speak. We have people flippantly attributing crazy
statements to God. Others tag their opinions with "God
said so and so." Even worse are the false "prophets" who
use His Name to manipulate people.

I'll say it again:

Authority flows through leadership—not around it.

While establishing my first church, my habit in prayer was
to pray, "God give me wisdom and insight to build this
church."

God would speak to me about every area of the church—
what I should preach, the staff, the Christian Education
department, the facilities, the finances, our property
expansion, the marketing, the music and even the women's
ministry. God answered my prayers and gave me specific
direction.

But then I went to work under a pastor at one of America's largest churches for a time. It was still my habit to pray, "God give me wisdom and insight about the church."

But God was silent. I would pray again and again, but I never got an answer. I was disturbed at the lack of response. I even considered that I might have missed God by coming on staff there and leaving my church in Mobile.

One day as I prayed, I asked God very specific questions about the church. Discouraged by the Lord's silence, I asked the senior pastor to lunch. As we were eating chips and salsa at our favorite Mexican dive restaurant, this pastor began to talk. As he did, he began to answer each and every one of the questions that I had prayed in secret that morning.

I leaned back and recognized the principle of authority at work.

> When Jesus had entered Capernaum, a centurion came to him, asking for help. "Lord," he said, "my servant lies at home paralyzed and in terrible suffering." Jesus said to him, "I will go and heal him." The centurion replied, "Lord, I do not deserve to have you come under my roof. But just say the word, and my servant will be healed. For I myself am a man under authority, with soldiers under me. I tell this one, 'Go,' and he goes; and that one, 'Come,' and he comes. I say to my servant, 'Do this,' and he does it." When Jesus heard this, he was astonished and said to those following him, "I tell you the truth, I have not found anyone in Israel with such great faith."
>
> Matthew 8:5-10

The centurion's response amazed Jesus. The soldier cared for the welfare of his servant enough to approach Jesus. He also respected the position that Jesus was in. Being a Jew, it would have been against Jewish law for Jesus to enter into the house of a Gentile. That's why the centurion said, "I don't deserve to have you come under my roof."

The centurion had faith that the Word of Jesus was applicable to his life. This man understood that authority flows *through* leadership—not around it.

Then the centurion used himself as an example of authority, "I'm a man under authority." He understood his position was in submission to the authority of Rome. He also pointed out that because he was *under* authority, he also possessed authority to speak commands. He said, "I give my men direction."

When you understand that you serve in authority under Jesus, you'll have confidence to lead others with boldness.

When I left the large church where I was under that senior pastor and founded another church of my own, I prayed, "Lord, give me wisdom and insight as to how to build this church." God began to speak to me again about every area.

POINTS FOR INCREASE:

Recruitment Vs. Volunteerism

Faith Vs. Need

Jesus does not expect us to work on empty. He equips those He recruits.

Communicate in simple terms.

Authority flows through leadership.

7 The Law Of Order

After David had constructed buildings for himself in the City of David, he prepared a place for the ark of God and pitched a tent for it. Then David said, "No one but the Levites may carry the ark of God, because the LORD chose them to carry the ark of the LORD and to minister before him forever."

I Chronicles 15:1-2

GOD IS A GOD OF ORDER.

All throughout Scripture, and as evidenced in Creation, we see that everything with God's Name on it has order, excellence and precision. Anything associated with Almighty God was made with infinite detail and was designed to function perfectly and in order.

King David learned the principles of *The Law Of Order* the hard way. After he had been enthroned as king of Israel, David wanted to bring the Ark of the Lord to Jerusalem. He instructed that a new cart be built in order to move the sacred cabinet. As the Ark was transported, people worshipped and celebrated with all their might. They made wonderful music as they journeyed.

Then tragedy struck. Uzzah irreverently reached out his hand to steady the Ark of God as the oxen pulling the cart stumbled. Immediately Uzzah died!

God had commanded that a human hand never touch the Ark. When God speaks a word—whether it's a command, a precept, a law or a principle—that word is established and cannot be overturned by emotion. No amount of sympathy can change God's Word. The Word must be exercised to the fullest extent, otherwise God would be proven a liar. Acting against the Word of God brings judgment.

Remember *The Law Of Hospitality: Do not treat as common what God inhabits.*

Instead of doing things the right way from the start, David became angry with God because of His seemingly irrational standard. So David refused to take the Ark to Jerusalem. Instead he left the Ark at the house of Obed-Edom.

David had the instruction of God's Word to obey! He had no right to be angry at God's judgment. David was wrong not to go to God's Word for instruction.

When God instructs us in His Word, we must obey it. Where there is no specific instruction, we should operate on principles that align with His Word.

After some time, David's anger subsided and he heard of the prosperity of the house of Obed-Edom because of the Ark. David carefully studied the proper way for the cart to be moved. He retrieved it to be brought to Jerusalem, instructing that the Ark be handled according to God's commands.

EXCELLENCE HONORS GOD.

As I travel, I see churches caught up in all kinds of activities. People are worshipping and celebrating, making music, yet their hands are reached out in irreverence.

To reverence means *to excel in honor* and *to acknowledge worth.* In the Book of Revelation, the four creatures and the twenty-four elders around the throne constantly extol the worth of God Almighty.

> *...Day and night they never stop saying: "Holy, holy, holy is the Lord God Almighty, who was, and is, and is to come." Whenever the living creatures give glory, honor and thanks to him who sits on the throne and who lives for ever and ever, the twenty-four elders fall down before him who sits on the throne, and worship him who lives for ever and ever. They lay their crowns before the throne and say: "You are worthy, our Lord and God, to receive glory and honor and power, for you created all things, and by your will they were created and have their being."* Revelation 4:8-11

Unfortunately, rather than ascribing holiness to the Lord, many Christians are very sloppy when it comes to their relationship with Him.

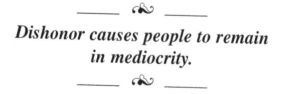

Dishonor causes people to remain in mediocrity.

You can witness disorder at the beginning of every church service, as people stroll in ten, fifteen—even thirty minutes late. In my opinion, that's not only rude to the God of Glory but it is actually offensive to Him. Skittish pastors are afraid to expect any better from their people. Tolerating such behavior actually does a disservice to a congregation, because dishonor causes people to remain in mediocrity.

God doesn't bless mediocrity!

Just before the 2000 Presidential Election, I had the opportunity to meet with George W. Bush, who was then Governor of Texas. In preparing for the meeting, I was told what time I was expected to arrive. Failure to be there at the appointed time would have been considered a great offense.

As important as that meeting was, it was much less important than my time scheduled with God!

If we're going to do something and stamp it with God's Name, we should do it with excellence. *Excellence is simply doing the right thing, the right way, at the right time.*

To hear some believers talk, you'd think that the anointing of God could only abide in a sloppy, disorganized place. That's about as far from the truth as you can get.

People admire excellence. People are drawn to excellence. People will pay for excellence.

I admire excellence without extravagance or waste.

Years ago, I visited the headquarters of Kenneth Copeland Ministries in Fort Worth, Texas. I was reluctant to go, because I had visited other headquarters of nationally-known ministries, all of which, I found extravagant in every way. This visit proved very different.

I was in Dallas at a meeting when I had a few extra hours of free time. My hobby is to visit churches and study them. So I set out to look at local church buildings and ministries.

When I arrived at Eagle Mountain (the church founded by Kenneth Copeland Ministries), I was impressed with the property immediately. I could see why Brother Copeland chose the beautiful sight to build his facilities there. When I approached the receptionist, she stood up and greeted me. When I mentioned that I was in town and just wanted to see the headquarters, she smiled and asked, "Have you had lunch yet?"

"No, I haven't," I replied.

"Would you please have lunch with us today?" she asked.

I readily accepted the offer, and within a couple of minutes, another woman escorted me to the staff cafeteria, through the buffet line and seated me with three ministers who served on the KCM staff.

During the lunch, the men inquired about my ministry. I must have asked a thousand questions about their operations, hoping to get some inside information. I was curious to learn about the fundamentals they operated by, their philosophy of ministry and the principles which guided them. Following the lunch, I was given a tour of every area of the headquarters including Kenneth and Gloria Copeland's offices.

The impression I went away with left me in awe of true excellence without extravagance. Every area of the facility was classy and demonstrated dignity with prudence.

The humility and servanthood I witnessed during my time there immediately dismissed all of the criticisms I had heard about that ministry down through the years. Excellence testified on their behalf that they not only honored the ministry, but also our God.

When I returned to my church, I did a walk through of our new facilities with my staff. We came up with four typed pages of things we should do before the next service. We began to see our facilities as visitors saw them. I began to expect excellence in every room.

I preached, *"If you see a piece of paper on the ground, you own it."* In other words, take ownership and pick it up.

CREATIVITY FLOWS FROM ACTION.

There were times when I felt uneasy about our progress as a church, so I would seek the Lord for creative ideas. I could sit, meditate the Word and think all day long, and nothing would come to my brain. Finally, if I didn't know what to do, I would just start cleaning, and suddenly, creative thoughts would flood my mind. The staff and I came up with all kinds of ideas which proved to serve our people better.

Now, when I travel to other churches as a consultant for pastors, it is not uncommon for us to find hundreds of things to do immediately.

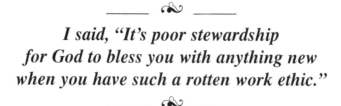

I said, "It's poor stewardship for God to bless you with anything new when you have such a rotten work ethic."

Recently, I was conducting a walk through at a facility with a large staff when I became disgusted. Every classroom was dingy, cluttered and drab. I couldn't imagine a child walking into those classrooms with any excitement or respect for the things of God. I rebuked the staff right then and there.

They had all kinds of excuses.

"So, these are the reasons that you use to justify living like this?" I chided.

One of the staff members in the group attempted to dissuade me. "We're going to build a brand-new building. Why should we spend so much time, effort and money on these old facilities?"

"For two reasons," I answered. "Number one: Because you don't deserve new facilities when you don't take care of the ones you have. Number two: Because it's poor stewardship for God to bless you with anything new when you have such a rotten work ethic."

That silenced the whole bunch.

Believe it or not, I was invited back to that church just a few months later to conduct another seminar.

This time I was surprised. The offices were organized and clean. The facilities were well kept and freshly painted. The rooms had been cleaned out. It was amazing.

God began to bless that church tremendously. Instead of taking the huge leap of faith required to build a new campus, they opted to trade facilities with another congregation in the city, doubling their square footage. It proved to be a win-win scenario for both parties.

By following the principles of order, they were able to turn their situation around and prepare their facilities for growth.

Out of respect for God and *The Law Of Order,* we are called to live at our best—to pursue excellence—to honor His Name.

> *The lazy man does not roast his game, but the*
> *diligent man prizes his possessions.*
> *Proverbs 12:27*

When you live in excellence, you celebrate what most people treat as common. You elevate everything in life as if it is something precious. You enjoy the blessings of God with great pleasure.

WE EITHER CREATE ORDER OR CAUSE DISORDER.

There is no middle ground here. You either create an environment of order with your actions, or you cause disorder by your lack of action.

Order can be defined as *the proper arrangement of resources.* Order creates an environment of expectation. People feel comfortable where there is order. They can relax and feel good.

> *For God is not a God of disorder but of peace. As in all the congregations of the saints...*
> *I Corinthians 14:33*

The atmosphere of order gives people peace. Disorder, on the other hand, causes strife and confusion. You can literally *feel* disorder. *(I don't know about you, but I can't stand being in a store where there is disorder. It's about the most uncomfortable place where you can be.)* People become very irritated in a disorganized place.

The direct opposite of order is *chaos.*

In the first verses of Genesis, the Bible declares that the earth was formless and empty—it was *chaotic.*

When the earth was in total chaos, God spoke to it. He immediately spoke, "Let there be light!" To create order, God first brought illumination to the chaos.

LIGHT IS THE TRANSFERENCE OF INFORMATION.

When God spoke to the chaos of the earth, He communicated light to the darkness and disorder. The entrance of God's Word brings light (Psalm 119:130).

Within the last few years, man has harnessed the ability to communicate through light. It is now the process by which the world communicates via the Internet, computers, telephones and other technology. Within light is the communication of knowledge.

Light reveals. Light illuminates. Light brings order.

In the beginning was the Word, and the Word was with God, and the Word was God. He was with God in the beginning. Through him all things were made; without him nothing was made that has been made. In him was life, and that life was the light of men. The light shines in the darkness, but the darkness has not understood it.   John 1:1-5

Darkness doesn't understand light. Light overwhelms darkness.

...God is light; in him there is no darkness at all.
I John 1:5

The entrance of God's light helps us reveal what is chaotic and in disorder. Many times we simply don't see our disorder. (It's a case of *"You can't see the forest for the trees."*) It often takes the Lord illuminating our understanding through the fresh eyes of others to see the chaos that we are living in.

When I consult businesses or churches with a walk through tour of their facilities or a review of their strategies, my unbiased observations simply bring to light what they may not have seen about themselves.

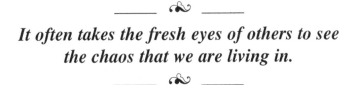

It often takes the fresh eyes of others to see the chaos that we are living in.

Recently, I began to consult with a national franchising company that stages homes for resale. Their sales pitch to realtors is that show homes sell much faster than empty ones. When prospective purchasers arrive in a home that has been "staged," they immediately are at ease and comfortable. They can see themselves living in that home.

Imagine. This company turns a profit by properly arranging things and creating order. Whether they know it or not, they're following a Scriptural principle.

God instructed Moses to carefully arrange the articles of furniture in the Tabernacle. Each article had a precise design and a specific place. The placement of the furniture inside the Tabernacle was modeled after the perfect design of Heaven itself (Hebrews 9).

When you put things in order in your life, you open the door for a progressive flow toward excellence and increase.

In the Tabernacle, the High Priest approached the presence of God with the proper protocol. Each step through its chambers prepared him for the next level. His strict adherence was vital in order to honor the presence of God.

In our lives, we should prepare for the presence of greatness. We should order our lives so that each step we take moves us toward excellence.

Esther was a young woman who was invited to the first pageant to marry a millionaire. Because of her beauty, she was selected to be one of only a few women who would have the opportunity to date King Xerxes.

Before going on their first date, Esther spent *twelve months* in beauty treatments and on a dietary program! That was excellence—the observance of protocol at its finest.

It's shameful that most people approach God with little or no preparation to enter His presence.

They spend *five minutes* in Scripture and *an hour* praying over stuff that's *not* Scriptural. I am convinced that we would be more effective in prayer, if we would spend the hour *preparing for prayer* in the Word, and then spend the five minutes praying.

When you honor the presence of God, you grow in excellence and you receive His divine favor to help you accomplish your dreams and desires.

Esther understood that the king had the power to grant her greatest desire—the salvation of her people. She approached him with the utmost respect, and as a result, an entire nation was spared from extinction.

When you create order, you create life.

(For more on Esther, go to www.NeilKennedyMinistries.com and look for my book "Faith For Favor," coming soon. For more on prayer, enter the keyword "prayer" for a free download.)

POINTS TO INCREASE:

God is a God of order.

Excellence honors God.

Creativity flows from action.

We either create order or cause disorder.

Light is the transference of information.

Grace To Grow

God gives us grace to grow. Grace is unmerited favor.

I think that sometimes we forget what it really means to receive unmerited favor. As children, we were accustomed to it. But as we grow older and are forced into the daily grind of working for a living, I think we sometimes forget the tremendous thrill of being given gifts we don't deserve.

My children certainly understand the principle of unmerited favor. On Christmas Eve, I can walk through the house and look into the bedrooms of each of my children and ponder the mess that a child can live in. Then the next morning, on Christmas Day, those same children will run in to the family room with unwavering expectation that they will receive gifts! *That's unmerited favor.*

> *But grow in the grace and knowledge of our Lord and Savior Jesus Christ.*   *II Peter 3:18a*

Peter tells us that we can grow in grace. We should all mature in the unmerited favor of God. Receiving blessing from the Lord is not something we earn by our works, but it's something we receive by grace.

Besides growing in grace, we are also supposed to grow in knowledge. I hope that *The Seven Laws Which Govern Increase And Order* have helped you to understand the principles that you need to walk in, in order to experience increase. But increase, in and of itself, isn't the prize you should be seeking. You must also seek to grow in grace.

Think of it this way. Jesus spent a short thirty-three years on this earth. He devoted just over three of those years to His earthly ministry. Then He entrusted His ministry to the hands of His followers.

Was Jesus worried?

No. In fact, He promised that His followers would do greater works than He had performed.

Greater works can only be done by His grace.

Before His departure, Jesus taught at length about the relationship that the Holy Spirit would have with us after Jesus was gone. He explained that the Holy Spirit would be sent to be *another* Counselor, Comforter and Teacher. He is *"another,"* in the same fashion and manner that Jesus was Counselor, Comforter and Teacher for His disciples during His earthly walk. The Holy Spirit works in unity with the Word. Just as Jesus spoke nothing on His own, the Spirit speaks nothing outside of the Word.

> *He said to them, "Go into all the world and preach the good news to all creation."*   Mark 16:15

Jesus commanded His disciples to "Go into all the world." This was a lofty command.

"Take on the world," He said. We hardly give this a second thought now, but think of the disciples hearing this statement from their perspective.

"We are only a few rough-hewn, working-class men. How can we accomplish this?" they probably asked.

I remember when God called me to plant my first church. The insecurity and insignificance that I felt was overwhelming. Each time I measured myself up against the task, I fell short.

It didn't help matters when I heard others mocking me for even thinking about doing such a thing. Seasoned ministers accused me of being arrogant. Peers laughed at my risk-taking mentality. Even some family members expressed their concerns that I was biting off more than I could chew.

FROM DREAMS TO REALITY

> *For you know the grace of our Lord Jesus Christ, that though he was rich, yet for your sakes he became poor, so that you through his poverty might become rich.*   *II Corinthians 8:9*

To make your dreams a reality, you must know that you have God's grace to supply your insufficiencies.

Moses received a command to lead his people out of bondage, yet he used his weaknesses as an excuse to argue with God. Moses didn't think he had the strength or the ability to lead God's people out of Egypt, yet Acts 7:22 tells us that Moses was *"mighty in words and in deeds"* (KJV).

Through the grace of God, the same rough-hewn disciples who struggled with post-crucifixion, pre-resurrection depression became the men who turned the world upside down. The global inversion was not accomplished by the elite of the day, by the educated or by the influential. It was accomplished by ordinary, unschooled men who had been with Jesus.

> *When they saw the courage of Peter and John and realized that they were unschooled, ordinary men, they were astonished and they took note that these men had been with Jesus.*   *Acts 4:13*

God's not interested in your excuses. His grace is sufficient to cover any of your shortcomings.

"But, what if I fail?"

So what if you do?

You should never fear failure. It is a wise man or woman who realizes that failure is not final.

The reward is worth the risk.

I have failed. In fact, I've failed ten times more than I have succeeded.

Though others may laugh and mock me, feeling superior from their comfortable positions of mediocrity, I have taken risks and I have reaped God's rewards. I've also discovered that any time you step out in faith, you will be challenged by elements of the status quo.

(For more information on the series, "From Dreams To Reality," go to www.NeilKennedyMinistries.com.)

WALKING ON WATER

> *During the fourth watch of the night Jesus went out to them, walking on the lake.   Matthew 14:25*

Jesus sent His disciples to cross the lake and to go on ahead of Him to Bethsaida. A storm buffeted their boat through the night. The disciples continued to row, but they were making no progress. The Bible says that Jesus saw them toiling but his intention was to walk right past them. He only stopped because they saw Him and were frightened.

When Peter recognized that it was Jesus out on the water, he said, "Lord, if it's really you, tell me to come."

Jesus said, "Come."

With that, Peter stepped out of the boat and began to walk on the water toward Jesus. Peter was fine until he began to consider the waves, the storm and his insufficiencies.

Jesus stepping forward to rescue Peter, asked, "Why did you doubt?"

There are rules for walking on water.

- Rule #1: Make sure Jesus is calling you to step out.

- Rule #2: Don't listen to those who stay in the boat.

- Rule #3: Once you're walking on the water, don't consider the natural elements which are against you.

The task God has given you can't be accomplished in the natural. The eighth principle of increase is different from the other Seven Laws. *Grace to grow is supernatural.*

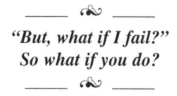

"But, what if I fail?"
So what if you do?

> *"But you will receive power when the Holy Spirit comes on you; and you will be my witnesses in Jerusalem, and in all Judea and Samaria, and to the ends of the earth."*   Acts 1:8

The work of the Holy Spirit in your life equips you with supernatural power to do what Jesus commands you to do. He gives you grace to grow.

Remember Albert Einstein's statement: "Nothing of great value is ever achieved without facing violent opposition."

In this life, you are rewarded by the problems that you solve. Problems exist until someone gets tired of them. The person who solves other people's problems is high in demand.

We are living in a wonderful period of time. The technology available to us, the "out-of-the-box" mentalities which capture men's imaginations, the new resources being discovered are all thrilling. The biggest frustration I have is when I see believers living below their levels of opportunity. It's very sad to see church people living in the nostalgia of yesteryear.

> *"...Who knows but that you have come to royal position for such a time as this?"*   Esther 4:14

As we step toward increase and order, we can be sure that God supernaturally gives us grace for our time. There is grace available to you that you will never receive, until you reach for the next level.

If you've ever looked back on something you've accomplished in life and said, "Wow, I never thought that I would get that done...." That's grace.

At every level and every turn, God's supernatural power and grace are yours just for the asking.

I have served in churches at every possible level and size—from volunteer to Senior Pastor—from no members to thousands. Following God requires grace for every level. I admire pastors who can take small churches and reach people in their towns, as much as I do those who have been charged with overseeing multiplied thousands. I believe that God does, too.

The key to accomplishing what God has equipped you to do is in having your confidence and significance based in Christ—not in your own personal successes.

Don't get me wrong. We *want* to win and we *will* win! But our significance must be based in God's grace. Apart from His working in our lives, success is shallow and empty. We are what we are though the grace and mercy of God.

In this, *grace to grow* is separate and distinct from any of the other *Seven Laws*. It isn't anything that we can do. **Grace to grow can be defined as the *supernatural momentum* that we receive from the Spirit of God.**

It's hard to explain, but when you have it, you know it. When you don't have it, you know it, too.

Grace to grow can also be defined as the favor of God in your life. Grace in your life is divinely connected to truth. Walking in truth (the knowledge of God's Word) leads you down the pathway of favor.

When Cain failed to worship God in truth—that is, according to what God had said—he fell into disfavor. The Lord said to him, "If you do what's right, won't you receive favor?" (Genesis 4:7)

Favor is a supernatural force that comes alongside your efforts. Favor opens doors, directs the course of leaders to promote you and causes the crowd to cheer your efforts.

But be warned!

The favor of God also attracts satanic attention. The devil directs his attacks toward anything that will halt your momentum. His aim is to undermine your success and to discredit your testimony. Your vision, your dream and your destiny will not come to you on a silver platter without violent forces opposing you.

You must fight the good fight of faith to see increase.

In order for *The Seven Laws Which Govern Increase And Order* to be fully operational in your life, you must understand that the grace of God—His supernatural favor— is yours for the asking. Remember: God isn't withholding anything *from* you. He's holding it *for* you.

It's God's good pleasure to bring you success and increase.

Are you willing to practice The Laws Of Increase And Order?

If you are, then I have a word for you from the Lord....

"Be fruitful and multiply!"

ABOUT THE AUTHOR

Neil Kennedy discovered *The Seven Laws Which Govern Increase And Order* out of necessity, from the principles he found in God's Word and from his own personal experience.

Neil worked as a heavy-machine operator in a coalmine in Oklahoma before attending Central Bible College in Springfield, Missouri, where he majored in Pastoral Studies. Working his way through college, Neil discovered that even his job as a salesman in a local carwash would give him insight into God's *Laws Of Increase.*

After finishing college and serving as a youth minister, Neil felt the Lord calling him to step out and pioneer Eastern Shore Christian Center in Mobile, Alabama. Growing the congregation from five people to 500, God then led Neil to step down from his position as Senior Pastor to become Executive Pastor at Church On The Move in Tulsa, Oklahoma. His experiences there allowed him to help develop the inner-workings of one of America's fastest-growing "mega- churches," where he was responsible for the entire pastoral care department, overseeing the needs of more than 10,000 members each week.

In 2001, armed with instruction from the Word and the practical knowledge he had gained, Neil once again felt the Lord directing him to pioneer a church. Obeying the Lord's call, he stepped out and founded Celebrate Family Church, in Orlando, Florida.

Neil's practical insight and straight-forward communication style have inspired thousands to take the necessary steps to realize their God-given potential. Neil's expertise makes him a highly-sought-after speaker and consultant to churches and businesses alike, and to anyone who wants to increase and achieve all that God has for them.

Neil now travels each week, ministering in churches and conducting *Grace To Grow Seminars* across America. Neil's burning desire is to challenge pastors, church congregations, and individuals to fulfill God's purposes for themselves, by using *The Seven Laws Which Govern Increase And Order.*

Neil has served on numerous boards, committees, and strategy forums, including the U.S. Missions Board, the Decade Of Harvest Task Force, the Evangelism Task Force, and the Dove-Award-winning musical group 4-Him.

The Ministry of Neil Kennedy, has the mission of teaching, equipping and funding church endeavors. His specialties include:

- Church Planting—developing and helping new works to go from the ground up,

- "Turn-Around" Churches—ministering to churches who've let tradition slow their momentum and find themselves irrelevant in today's world, and

- "Next-Level" churches—assisting pastors who, for whatever reason, have hit a barrier in their growth they just can't seem to break through.

Neil has also helped launch an e-marketing company, called "ChurchTour 360," which aids churches in developing positive public relations images in their communities.

Neil and his wife, Kay, have three children, Alexandra, Chase, and Courtney, and they reside in Fairhope, Alabama.

For more information, or to schedule Neil Kennedy for a meeting, please visit www.NeilKennedyMinistries.com.